Praise for *The Shadow of Evil*

The Shadow of Evil is a son's critical exa..... death and his passionate and eloquent assessment of the psychology spiritual values necessary for healing. This book is a superb resource and "mandatory" reading for victims, family members, trauma specialists, and anyone challenged by traumatic life events. A personal pilgrimage as well as an educational and spiritual treasure.

Jane Crisp, Division of Victim Assistance, State of South Carolina

I have read many books dealing with violence, but this book is unique because it speaks to the tough question of where God is in the lives of victims of violence. A must for anyone struggling with this issue.

Nancy Ruhe-Munch, former executive director, Parents of Murdered Children, Inc., Cincinnati, Ohio

How does one face the senseless murder of a loved one? How do we confront our ideas of fairness, justice, our faith, and the character of God? These issues Jeff faces with tremendous compassion and personal understanding. I recommend this book to anyone who has lived these questions or who works with people in this pain.

Russ Phillips, MA, licensed mental health counselor, licensed marriage and family therapist, Orlando, Florida

The grief, the suffering of survivors, and the questioning of one's beliefs are put into a true perspective by this book. The insight and personal experience of Jeff... exudes true caring and guidance for other victims and families... this book is the outcome that can help everyone who suffers from a critical incident.

Gary W. Tabor, former captain, Wichita Police Department, Wichita, Kansas

ISBN 978-1-64114-699-9 (paperback)
ISBN 978-1-64114-700-2 (digital)

Christian Faith Publishing, Inc.
832 Park Avenue
Meadville, PA 16335
www.christianfaithpublishing.com

Printed in the United States of America

After my son was murdered, I was devastated. After reading this book, I knew I was going in the right direction, as many of the feelings expressed here are the same feelings I was having. It has given me much comfort in a healthy and uplifting way.

Corinne Radke, founder, Wichita chapter, Parents of Murdered Children

This is truly a work which should help survivors, victims and all those who care about our world today. I look for it to have a major impact upon the entire victim community.

Carol Kaloger, former chapter coordinator, Parents of Murdered Children, Deltona, Florida

The Shadow of Evil by Jeffrey M. Davis deals with one of society's most problematic issues, namely, 'where *is* God in a violent world?' The great value of this contribution to the subject is that its author, besides being academically and spiritually qualified to write on the subject, also brings the experience of having been personally, severely victimized by violence. As one who educates religious leadership on crime victimization, I highly recommend this book to anyone concerned about this vital issue.

David W. Delaplane, executive director, the Spiritual Dimension in Victim Services, Denver, Colorado

This first work by Mr. Davis gives a very personal and yet accurate picture of the difficulties faced by survivors of violent crime—from the first indication that something is wrong through the painful aftermath and the continual struggle to heal.

Ellen T. Hanson, former chief of police, Lenexa, Kansas

As I read *The Shadow of Evil,* I was amazed at how many times Jeffrey M. Davis's words reflected the identical feelings that I had experienced as a victim of violent crime. The author's interpretation of God's part in the victimization process was poignant.

Kathleen Finnegan, director/spokesperson, Florida Stop Turning Out Prisoners

THE
SHADOW
OF
EVIL

Where Is God in a Violent World?

Jeffrey M. Davis

NOTE FROM THE AUTHOR

When I first conceived the idea of writing edition 1 of this book over twenty years ago, I hoped to accomplish three things. First, I wanted this work to serve as a tribute to my mother. Her death was tragic and senseless, but I could not allow it to be meaningless; I refused to accept that she died in vain. I knew it had been my mother's nature all her life to take up for the underdog and reach out to those in need, and I made it my mission to do that for her with this book. I recognized that by using her story to assist others who have endured their own adversity and heartache, her loving and giving nature could live on and provide some meaning to her death.

My second objective was to ensure that this book remain as timeless as possible by examining enduring themes, not focusing on fleeting, contemporary concerns. The emotions of doubt, worry, grief, guilt, frustration, loneliness, regret or fear, along with so many others, have always been part of our human nature and always will be. Therefore, it has been my intent from the outset to share my emotional struggles in a way that would be helpful to others dealing with similar feelings. I believe that coming to grips with these emotions remains as necessary today as it was twenty years ago.

People suffer loss through all forms of tragedy on this earth, not just through violence, as in my case. Loss can be experienced through divorce, illness, accidents, bankruptcy, and all other sorts of painful misfortune. So for this reason, this book is not intended to speak solely to those surviving violence. Instead, I hope that anyone who has suffered adversity of any nature will find solace in reading my story, and come to see my struggles as similar to their own. This was my third objective.

So if you choose to read my story, realize that you will not find the emotional journey you are embarking upon to be an easy or painless one. Nor will you find a neatly packaged "all is well" conclusion at the end. Instead, you will likely share many of my painful experiences, feel my turbulent mix of emotions, experience the difficulty of challenging long-held assumptions, and you may even find yourself questioning God's presence and purpose in your life through it all.

But it is my overriding hope that as a result of your walking down this road with me, you will emerge on the other side with a better acceptance of what you have been through, a greater understanding of who you are, and a sense of hope and renewal, with a brighter perspective of your own tomorrow.

In Remembrance

To the memory of my mother, Dolores Davis, whose tragic death inspired me to undertake this endeavor. Her senseless murder has left an aching void in my life, which will never be filled. It has also deprived this world of a wonderful and loving person. Still, if even one person benefits from reading this book, I know her death will not have been in vain. Mom, until we meet again in the world that knows no pain or suffering, I will love and miss you always.

Where Are You Now

Maybe I took for granted
You'd be around
To pick me up on my way down
I thought my feet were planted
Firmly on the ground
'Til one day my whole world came unwound
And like a ball of yarn
Kept neatly on a spool
You held the life together
Of this brokenhearted fool
And what once was the exception
Now seems to be the rule
And there's a burnin' question
A fire in my mind
You always had the answers
the ones I couldn't find
So all I'm askin'
Is, "Where are you now?"

CONTENTS

PREFACE

Life acquaints us all at one time or another with its harsher realities. Sometimes adversity creeps subtly into our lives as a business slides into bankruptcy, or as a once-meaningful relationship dies. Tragedy may strike with a doctor's call concerning our latest chest x-ray, or with a policeman at the door saying that our child has been involved in a car accident. One of life's few certainties is that eventually we will all taste the bitterness of personal loss, regardless of its nature.

Some of us, though, have experienced tragedy involving an act of violence directed against ourselves or our loved ones that will forever alter our lives. As a result of such evil, we realize that we will never be the same again. Much of what we had taken for granted has been brought into question: our perspective of the world, our sense of identity, our values, our self-esteem, our feeling of personal security, even our faith in God.

We struggle with haunting questions:

What could I have done to prevent this?

Why did my son have to die?

How can a loving God permit these things to happen?

Why did I leave my wife alone?

What would motivate someone to do this?

Why couldn't it have been someone else?

Where was God when my daughter was raped?

Why couldn't I have been there to prevent my son's death?

Where is God now that I need Him most?

We don't fully comprehend what is happening, and neither do our friends and family; nonetheless, it is the predominant reality in our lives.

13

You may have found, as I have, that these questions of circumstance and doubts of faith are even more frightening than the violence that originally touched your life.

Adversity, evil, violence, and death are nothing new to mankind. We've been living with them since God first breathed life into man. No doubt we will continue to battle against them until Christ returns. So this book is unique only in that it attempts to address violence in a very pointed and personal manner—by looking at the emotional and spiritual toll it takes on its victims.

Moreover, my intention for this book is that anyone who has suffered adversity, endured tragedy, or asked the haunting questions of *Why?* to so many of life's unfair and often-unexplained circumstances will be helped by reading it. Many people whose opinions I trust have found this to be so. From whatever perspective you may be approaching this book as a reader, my hope is that you find here an accurate account of your daily struggle to overcome the trauma inflicted on you by cruel circumstances.

If you have not yet been victimized directly, you could easily be next. You might send your daughter off to school one day and never see her again. You could eventually find yourself facing a psychopath pointing a gun at your head. Or you may simply begin to realize that you just can't trust people anymore.

Some of you may have already become victims and will carry the emotional and physical scars for the rest of your lives. Perhaps you were the innocent victim of a drive-by shooting who got in the way of a stray bullet. Maybe you have been the victim of severe spousal abuse and are terrorized by the thought that your estranged husband will return to finish what he started. You may even have been shot and left for dead by an armed robber who wanted to leave no witnesses behind.

Others of you, like myself, are not technically victims of violence at all. We haven't suffered personal injury, so we don't meet the legal criteria to even be considered victims. Still, we have indeed been victimized in our own way. We experience the daily hell of knowing that someone we love has been injured or killed by the violent, malicious actions of another person. We constitute the *invisible victims* of violence in our society—the forgotten survivors of violent crime who aren't counted in the statistics, but who suffer emotionally just as much as do the legally recognized victims.

The impact resulting from these innumerable acts of violence is the central focus of this work. Since in this context all of us who have been touched by violence are both its *victims* and its *survivors*, I will use these terms interchangeably throughout this book.

We survivors are a widely diverse group, because violence plays no favorites. Young and old, male and female, rich and poor, black and white are all vulnerable. Over 5 million people in this country experience the consequences of violence every year.[1] In fact, if a memorial wall were erected to honor all those who were killed by an act of homicide over the last twenty years, it would contain over 360,000 names and measure six times longer than the Vietnam War Memorial.[2]

To be sure, this is a difficult and painful topic—one that most people would rather not talk or read about. Still, it cannot be ignored. Those of you who are victims yourselves and those of us who are the family and friends of victims can't ignore the pain. We can no longer remain silent about the chaos that it inflicts. We need to admit our fears, vent our frustrations, express our anger, confess our bitterness, own up to our guilt, and come to grips with our depression and despair.

The problem is that too many of our friends, and even family, don't want to listen to us. We make them uncomfortable. They don't know what to say or how to react. We remind them of the fragility of life, its cheapness in our world today, and of their own vulnerability in a violent society.

Besides, according to many people, we are at the point now that it's time to "get on with our lives." We "can't continue to dwell on what happened" because our loved ones "would want us to go on." And of course, we should "leave the past in the past" for the sake of our futures. Those of you who have been devastated by violence have heard these clichés from well-meaning family and friends to the point of exasperation.

You seek help from those you trust and often can't find it. That is why I have written this book—I hope it will be helpful to you.

I must caution you at this point, however: If you are looking for pat answers, you won't find any. If you expect to read here that good ultimately prevails over evil, you won't, because I don't believe that myself (not prior to the Second Coming, at least). I can't even offer you the reassurance that we will get answers to all our tormenting questions in this lifetime, because usually, that won't happen.

Therefore, this book is anything but an idealistic attempt to explain away agonizing issues and tormenting questions with happily-ever-after references to better days ahead. It simply represents the thoughts of one who, just like yourself, struggles every day with the aftermath of crushing adversity in his own life.

I have simply endeavored to share my feelings, thoughts, and experiences on this subject with you. My hope is to provide you with some insights into your questions, validate your turbulent emotions, and perhaps help you get a better handle on your own shaken faith in God. I share my story, hopeful that in so doing, I can demonstrate to you who are fighting the same battles I am that you are not alone. I want other survivors to know that there are people who do understand what violence means to its victims and who can empathize with their never-ending ordeal of trying to regain control of their lives.

While we will live the rest of our days wrestling with the stigma that violence has placed upon us, I believe we still have cause for hope. We can admit that we are indeed different people because of what has happened to us, but we must focus now on what our future will be in light of what we have endured.

Will our future be one of emptiness, cynicism, isolation, bitterness, and regret, or will we be able to move past our despair into a lifestyle that offers some sense of purpose and renewed desire to overcome our tragedy? While only God knows each of our futures, it is my hope that as the reader, you will be able to share my experiences, relate to where I have been in my grief, recognize my emotional turmoil as similar to yours, and eventually see some glint of light at the end of this tunnel of darkness.

PART I

The Descent into Darkness

Nothing good ever comes of violence.

—Martin Luther

For violence inevitably attracts morally inferiors.

—Albert Einstein

Violence… disruption… disorder… strike
at the freedom of every citizen.

—Commission on Civil Disorder, 1968

The violence done us by others is often less painful
than that which we do to ourselves.

—François de La Rochefoucauld

CHAPTER 1

THE CATASTROPHE THAT
COULDN'T HAPPEN

For if a man lives many years, let him rejoice in them all,
but let him remember that the days of darkness will be many.

—Ecclesiastes 11:8

The day in January that marked the end of life as I'd known it for thirty-nine years began uneventfully. Just the day before, I had resigned my position as a management development coordinator with a large defense company to go into business for myself. This was to be my first day as an independent business man, and I wanted to make the transition a good one.

I spent the morning attending to all those accumulated personal details I hadn't gotten around to the last couple of weeks: paying bills, dropping books off at the library, working around the house, registering my eleven-year-old for Little League, and the big project—cleaning out the garage. In addition to developing my new management consulting business, my other business priority for 1991 was expanding the lawn maintenance service I had started a couple of years prior. That required more equipment, which demanded more space, which meant overhauling the garage. I was determined to make the most of every inch of space out there, and so I spent most of the afternoon reorganizing.

In addition to my thoughts of transition in lifestyle, I was maintaining an attentive ear to the radio. The Gulf War had begun three days before, and I was very interested in which direction that conflict was headed. The day sped by fairly rapidly as I engulfed myself in work and thoughts of what this new year would bring.

As I recall, it was somewhere around 5:30 p.m. when the phone rang. I remember the carpet sales representative had just left after finalizing the adjustment we received to replace carpet ruined by vandalism a few weeks prior. When my wife, Nan, motioned me to the phone, I grudgingly took the receiver from her, irritated because I still had work to do in the garage and didn't have time for socializing. She mouthed the words *This is important*, and the concerned look on her face told me I'd better soften my approach a little.

I heard my sister Laurel's voice on the line. Since she lived in Denver, Colorado, and I was in Orlando, Florida, we didn't get to talk often. I was glad to hear from her even though I was still preoccupied with my unfinished chores. Laurel said something about receiving a call from our mother's friend in Wichita, Kansas. This friend had been contacted by the Sedgwick County Sheriff's Office earlier that day. Laurel then said something about Mother's house being burglarized.

I was off balance and searching for the bottom line when my mouth went to cotton as she stammered, "Someone threw a brick through the patio door, and Mother's missing".

The most haunting aspect of that conversation was hearing her voice break as she said the word *missing*. Still, she was doing her best to remain calm, which was more than I could say for myself.

Anger began to build within me even then as I envisioned what might have happened. I was already asking myself how much adversity one person could stand. My family was still reeling from the effects of severe damage to our home caused by vandals out to terrorize my daughter just two weeks earlier. Someone had violated our home, and now someone else had burglarized my mother's. I was furious at my helplessness to do anything about either.

My mind raced with possibilities as Laurel related more details: no sign of valuables missing, car still in the driveway, the front door locked, the rear patio glass door shattered, both phones pulled from the jacks, exterior telephone lines cut, sheets and comforter missing from the bed. As a lifelong pessimist and hardened ex-police officer, every ounce of intuition within me screamed this was bad—really bad.

Still, I was struggling against fear to see logic, to look at the situation in a way that made sense. Nothing of value taken indicated to me that it wasn't just a burglary. The noise that inevitably accompanies shattered glass meant that someone probably came in when she wasn't there.

Three haunting questions, however, indicated the worst. If she wasn't there when the crime occurred, why was the car still in the driveway? Why were the sheets gone from the bed, and what purpose would they serve? And worst of all, what was the significance of the severed phone wires?

I besieged Laurel with an onslaught of questions. When was she notified? Who had called the police? Who else knows? Who found the house the way it was? What were the police doing at that point? I struggled to contain the panic creeping up around me by gathering as much information as possible. Uncertainty has always been threatening to me, and in this case, I wanted all the information I could get to help me reason through what this might represent.

We talked about half an hour, then hung up after exhausting all the questions we could ask each other. We left it that she would call me back once she had talked to the sheriff's office and had contacted Mother's brother and sisters.

As soon as I hung up, Nan asked what was wrong, but my panic and rage permitted me only to offer a disjointed summary of our conversation. Reality had already begun to assume a surrealistic nature. Time seemed to stop, and everything else suddenly became insignificant. I kept visualizing my mother's house as I fought off the images of catastrophe that seeped around the edges of my consciousness.

***

We are constantly bombarded with incidents of violence in the United States today. Our morning newspaper describes the execution of three youths by a masked gunman who robbed a fast-food restaurant. We watch the anchor on the evening news tell us how rioters dragged a driver from his vehicle and savagely kicked him to near death. We listen as the radio news relates the details of several unsolved murders that indicate the actions of a serial killer. We hear about dozens of children who have been sexually assaulted by preschool staff members over a period of years. Most recently, we even hear a new phrase being used—recreational murder—to describe killing someone simply for the fun and excitement of it.

Violence has become so pervasive and random in the last few decades that we have become desensitized to it. Our lives are so saturated with stories of crime, injury, destruction, and death that we lose sight of the personal havoc it inflicts on its victims. For the most part, we compartmentalize these incidents into our consciousness by regarding them as just another tragic aspect of life, one to which we want to believe we are immune.

However, reality often dictates much to the contrary, because none of us is exempt from the violence that surrounds everyone in our world. As much as we might like to deny it, statistically, we are all at risk. In the United States alone: one woman is battered every fifteen seconds,[1] two people die every hour at the hands of a drunk driver,[2] 1,800 people are robbed every day, over 21,000 people are violently assaulted each week, and nearly 9,000 women are raped every month.[3] Each year, nearly 25,000 names are added to the list of homicide victims in this country,[4] which equates to one person being murdered here every twenty-two minutes. Some source experts estimate that between 200 and 300 serial killers are currently active within the United States.[5]

Even the financial implications of this carnage are staggering. It is estimated that the average career criminal commits between 187 and 287 crimes per year. With each crime costing approximately $2,300, the activities of a single career criminal can cost society over $400,000 per year.[6]

Violence is often just waiting for the right set of circumstances to unleash its consequences. You are in a hurry and take a shortcut through a bad part of town. You get complacent and decide to jog after dark. You irritably honk at the wrong car without thinking. Maybe you didn't do anything and just happened to be in the wrong place at the wrong time.

As too many of us already know, once we become a statistic of violence, our world changes forever. For some, those changes are relatively subtle. Somehow you just don't feel comfortable after dark anymore; you don't take a vacation for fear of leaving your house unattended; you now keep your door locked at home, even in the middle of the day.

For others, your lives have been altered in a more insidious manner. Maybe you are a child molestation victim who has come to realize that you won't ever be able relate to the opposite sex in a meaningful way. Possibly you lost your parents to a drunk driver, and your despair and depression since have cost you a marriage and a career. Perhaps your son was abducted and murdered, and years later you feel abandoned by your friends who act as if he never existed by refusing to mention his name.

Unfortunately for those of us who are the survivors of violence, we carry the dubious distinction of being source experts on the emotional devastation it leaves. Being the survivor of a homicide victim means nothing but grief, I know from experience. I long for the days when my only exposure to violence and death was secondhand. Because of the actions of one homicidal psychopath, however, I will spend the rest of my life learning to live with the terrible realities of losing someone I loved to murder.

While the epidemic proportions of violence in this country may be unprecedented, the evil it represents has been with us for thousands of years. The most notable story of its effects on one individual is found in the biblical book of Job.

We are told that Job was a devout and righteous man, unconditionally committed to the ways of God. He had been blessed by God throughout his life, and was considered to be one of the richest and most prosperous men of his time. Satan recognized this and targeted him for evil, believing that when Job suffered catastrophe, he would renounce his faith and give up on God. For some reason known only to God, He allowed the devil his plan and let Job be subjected to numerous calamities, one of which was the loss of all his sons and daughters (Job 1:13-19).

Picture Job tending to his chores one uneventful morning when a servant comes rushing in to tell him that all his children have just been killed. With no warning or suspicion, Job is told that his family has just been wiped out. Probably in his middle age, Job had no doubt invested his lifetime in these children. He had shared in their births, played with them as toddlers, helped them with their schoolwork, counseled them with their problems, and given his daughters away at their weddings. His life was their lives, and then they were gone in an instant.

The agony he must have felt at realizing he had lost his entire family, along with all his material assets, is one that most people can only imagine. Still, we survivors can speculate that his initial reaction might have mirrored our own.

At first, he probably thought, *There must be some mistake. This can't be happening. These things happen to other people, but surely not to me.* The shock and refusal to accept this horror probably overshadowed everything else at that moment. Perhaps once he was convinced of the reality of the situation, he began asking *why. Why did this have to happen to my kids and not someone else? This isn't right. They didn't deserve to die. They were too young.* What bitter anguish these questions represent to those who have asked them.

He probably experienced an inexpressible frustration once he realized that all his calamities were simply the act of inexplicable evil against him. Deadly acts of destruction had been directed at him and those he loved for no apparent reason.

He must have fought against accepting at a heart-level the dreadful reality that evil exists everywhere in this world and exercises its will as it chooses. His family died futile deaths for no conceivable purpose.

Job's thoughts, unfortunately, are not recorded; and any inferences we might make are pure speculation. The Bible simply quotes him as saying, "Naked I came from my mother's womb, and naked I shall return; the Lord gave and the Lord has taken away; blessed be the name of the Lord" (Job 1:21). Admirably, he even went on to rhetorically ask himself, "Shall we receive good at the hand of God, and shall we not receive evil?" (Job 2:10).

When we are confronted with a life catastrophe of such unprecedented proportion today, our initial reaction is similarly quite often denial. You may have said to yourself, *This can't be happening to me. I'm just on my way to the store, and now some maniac is telling me to give him my car or he'll shoot me.* Perhaps upon hearing that your loved one had been murdered, you reacted with, *That can't be true, I just talked to her on the phone a few hours ago. She can't be dead.*

Those of you who have shared similar circumstances recognize the threat to your mental stability that this type of news represents. You experience a state of disbelief at the possibility that you could actually be facing a situation that most people only read about in the newspapers or watch on television. The thought of someone you love being kidnapped, assaulted, or murdered is so foreign to anything you have ever experienced that your conscious mind refuses to accept it. Because you have become so accustomed to hearing about the violence in our society, you have learned to tune it out. It has had no sense of reality at all—until that moment when it crashes down upon you personally.

***

In my case, the worst was only implied at that point. It had yet to become reality. Therefore, I found myself using a number of rationalizations to explain away the circumstances, even though I probably didn't believe them myself. *She must have gone someplace to get help. Maybe she is hurt and at one of the hospitals. She is alive, but being held against her will. She'll probably call soon and tell us where she is.*

All my prior police experience told me these were lies, however. Because the fact is that when someone is missing from a burglarized home for several hours, that person has probably either been kidnapped or killed. To accept this reality, however, meant that my life as I knew it was over. My mother was a source of stability for me. She offered hope when I was depressed. She always looked for the good side when all I could see was the bad. Her voice on the telephone was a stabilizing influence when I felt things were slipping out of control.

I knew even then that if I lost her to this kind of madness, the cynical, hardened part of my nature I had tried for so long to overcome would dominate my future. So I kept telling myself lies as the evening hours crawled by and I waited for the phone to ring.

CHAPTER 2

THE EVIL SURROUNDING
US ALL

Destruction and violence are before me…
For the wicked surround the righteous,
so justice goes forth perverted.

—Habakkuk 1:3, 1:4

We've all read stories in the newspaper about children who were abducted, leaving their parents to endure years of agony not knowing if their kids were still alive. One nationally renowned case involved the disappearance of a six-year-old girl from a quiet neighborhood in Wilkinsburg, Pennsylvania. Her parents undoubtedly endured untold hell for sixteen months until her body was finally discovered the following year.[1]

Perhaps upon reading of similar circumstances you have asked yourself, *How could anyone live with that kind of terror? What would it be like not knowing if someone you love is dead or alive?*

For fourteen days after I first learned of my mother's disappearance, I discovered in a very personal way how overwhelming this experience can be.

After dozens of fruitless long-distance phone calls late into that night of January 19, I finally resolved that nothing else could be done and crawled into bed. Uncertainty consumed my mind as I lay there with sleep eluding me. Never in my life had any fear been more terrifying or any uncertainty more agonizing.

I kept replaying in my head our family's Christmas visit to my mother's house in rural Sedgwick County, Kansas, just a few weeks before. The image of her warm smile as she greeted us at the front door wouldn't leave my mind. I could see her house with her Christmas tree brightly decorated and the lights strung over the frozen rosebushes outside. I remembered my brother-in-law and me grilling hamburgers one cold evening out on the patio. I saw my kids romping in the snow with our dog the day before Christmas. I remember the roast turkey we had all enjoyed the night before we left. I was haunted by Mother's good-bye hug and words of caution before we started out in the snow on our trip home.

What caused my blood to run cold, though, was trying to envision the nameless, faceless evil responsible for this nightmare. Her house, nestled among the wheat fields of the pastoral Kansas countryside, had once seemed so peaceful and friendly. Now in my mind it was a secluded, frightening place, hiding some evil secret that hung on the cold night air. What had just three weeks before been a warm home filled with joking and laughter was now an empty, silent tomb cordoned off by yellow police crime scene tape. An unseen, sinister presence pervaded the whole setting in my mind, making the entire situation too horrible to accept.

Perhaps you too have experienced the desperation I felt. You needed to do something, anything, but the fate of your loved one rested in the hands of someone else's. The police became the agents of action, and you were suddenly relegated to the role of observer. You wanted information, facts, reassurance; but all you found were more unanswerable questions.

Your sense of panic and helplessness became almost greater than the horror that confronted you. You had spent your entire life believing that you were in control of your destiny. As captain of your own ship, you really believed that you could handle whatever came your way. Then one hideous set of circumstances forced you to realize just how little influence you actually do have over your own world.

You had become comfortable with the illusion that everything in your life was in order, neat, and logical with few loose ends. In your mind, violent crime was something you had only read or heard about. Your lifestyle put you at low risk for the kinds of things that happen out on the street. You had your home alarm system, your security lighting, and the police were just a 9-1-1 call away.

After all, you had always reminded yourself, where could you be safer than in your own home? How could this madness be? You searched relentlessly, just as I did, for some explanation for the insanity threatening your life. You searched frantically... and found nothing.

***

As the days following Mother's disappearance dragged on in maddening slowness, my entire world became consumed with thoughts of her. All else in my life ceased to exist. I gave little thought to the lawn being days past my meticulous maintenance schedule. I didn't care if the car wasn't washed as it normally would have been. I even forgot a few business details that would have constituted a global crisis just a few days before. I became aware of how these seemingly paramount matters were now no more than trivia in comparison to what was really important to me.

Minutes crawled by like hours, hours became days, and each day was a lifetime. I began to question how much longer I could survive this slow-motion hell.

I spent every waking hour trying to explain what the facts as I knew them could mean. All my deductions still came down to the same few possibilities. Someone who knew her wanted to harm her, for some obscure reason. It was a random act where she happened to be the victim of a burglary gone awry. Or she had been stalked and murdered by a psychotic killer.

The more I considered this case, the more terror I felt. It was obvious to me even at this point that this had been no random act. Whoever had done this had methodically planned, carried out, and concealed his actions.

Because I had once been a police officer, the sheriff's office treated me very well and often disclosed more information than they normally would have. Still, three separate crime scene searches of her residence revealed little evidence. The normal missing persons' alerts had turned up nothing. Her missing purse and small personal items had failed to surface.

The fact was, they had precious little to go on; and in the back of my mind, I was beginning to understand why. I was slowly coming to the conclusion that my mother had been killed by a psychopath who took her life to fulfill some murderous fantasy.

Regardless of how I envisioned this scenario ultimately unfolding, I was constantly tormented with the question, Why my mother? Why her and not one of the 300,000 other people around her? Why her house and not one of the neighbors? Why that particular night? What reason would anyone have to take the life of a total stranger?

My experience with other survivors leads me to believe that when we are confronted with this type of threat to our reality, we almost immediately begin asking the first in a lifetime of *why*'s expressed universally by victims of crime. I believe this is a direct result of our conscious minds striving to make order out of chaos.

These traumas are so threatening to our entire perspective of the world that our intellectual being simply cannot accept the circumstances at face value. Therefore, we find ourselves struggling for logical reasons to explain irrational actions.

We search for a reason by asking ourselves such rhetorical questions as What did I do to deserve this? Why my daughter? Why did it have to happen to my son?

I have heard homicide survivors agonize for years over these same questions that I have asked myself hundreds of times.

As a Christian, I have always believed that I understood the implications of the free will that God has granted all of us. He allows us to make our own decisions, so we live our lives for good or for evil based upon the choices we make. At an intellectual level, this fit my neatly arranged perspective of the world.

Now that I have personally had to confront the full consequences of the evil that resulted in my mother's death, however, my understanding of self-determination is much more personal. I am now painfully aware of how devastating the gift of free will can be to those of us who have been victimized by the abuse of it.

Granted, we can cite countless examples of the good that man has chosen to do for his fellow man. We hear daily about selfless acts of courage in times of natural disaster and war. Some people dedicate their entire lives to working for the benefit of others, as seen in people like Mother Teresa, Martin Luther King, Jonas Salk, and Billy Graham. The most obvious example of selfless free will that altered the entire course of mankind was the submission of Christ to death for the sake of man's sinfulness.

Still, the names Adolf Hitler, Saddam Hussein, Jeffrey Dahmer, John Gacy, Charles Manson, and Ted Bundy remind us that man's ego, avarice, and cruelty continue to result in the destruction of thousands of innocent lives today.

The book of Genesis attributes the original exercise of free will to Adam and Eve. God had given them everything they would need to live a carefree, eternal existence in the garden of Eden with Him. However, when confronted by the devil, the father of all evil, they were easily talked into going against God's will and doing the one thing He prohibited (Gen. 3:1-7). Biblically speaking, their actions sealed our fate. We have lived with the reality of sin in this world and its impact on our lives ever since.

In all this time, God has continued to allow us to make our own choices, all the while knowing that these may ultimately lead to our destruction or of those around us.

Man's inhumanity to his fellow man can be seen in this context as simply another perversion of this freedom of choice. If people choose the exploitation, intimidation, and destruction of others as a way of life, God allows these travesties because to do otherwise would be to make us robots, blindly submitting to His will. God determined at the outset of His relationship with man that He would "will" Himself to be powerless over man's evil actions rather than force our obedience.[2] Intellectually, this makes sense to most people.

But to the survivor of violence sorting through the emotional debris of their life, an emotional acceptance of this precept is ineffably hard to grasp.

While violence has many faces today, the people who most often practice it are known as sociopaths (sometimes referred to as psychopaths). Simplistically speaking, these are people who will commit any evil necessary to further their own purposes. As characterized by the mental health diagnosis of antisocial personality disorder, the sociopath lives in a world of lies, deceit, manipulation, opportunism, megalomania, victimization of others, and, many times, violence.

Not all sociopaths are violent, but nearly all habitually violent people are sociopathic. Since they have little conscience, they have no regard for how their actions will impact the lives of their victims. The violent criminal is consumed with ensuring self-gratification at all costs, at the expense of anyone else, by whatever means he determines necessary.

Regardless of their criminal expertise—be it rape, assault, robbery, murder, or other crimes—sociopaths share several very significant characteristics. For one, they all view other people merely as objects, dehumanized entities to be used for their own exploitation. A burglar or a robber sees people only in terms of what degree of wealth they represent, existing solely to be used for his benefit. The rapist sees a woman only as the object of his own obsession with control over another, someone to be overpowered to prove his dominance. The serial murderer sees other people only from the perspective of those who might represent one more outlet for the sexual fantasy that dominates his life.

The antisocial personality characteristically evidences a tremendous amount of rage toward society. From childhood on, these people establish a very distorted perspective of the world through which they see themselves as superior to everyone else, and therefore entitled to whatever they want. They feel no sense of obligation to others close to them or to society in general. They habitually blame everyone around them for their own problems and usually act out their anger (in the form of various criminal acts) against anyone whom they perceive as a means to their given ends.[3]

This attitude of contempt for society generates an insatiable need for antisocial personalities to exert power, dominance, and control over other people. They will go to any means to manipulate, exploit, abuse, or humiliate people simply to demonstrate their own superiority. Interviews with convicted serial murderers, in particular, have revealed startling information in this respect. Nearly all have stated that once they have actually carried out their murderous fantasies by killing someone and gotten away with it, they assume a very superior attitude toward other people. Many of these killers admit that as they continue their murders successfully, they come to see themselves as almost immortal. They have committed every sort of atrocity for long periods of time without recrimination and believe, in their minds, that they have actually become gods.

Psychopaths also delude themselves into believing that the victim is the source of blame, as evidenced in such statements as, "If he hadn't left the keys in the car, I wouldn't have stolen it," "If she hadn't walked home alone in the dark, I wouldn't have attacked her," or "If he hadn't said to me what he did, I wouldn't have killed him."

In an excellent exposé on criminal behavior, Stanton Samenow describes how one sociopath justified shooting a man during the course of one of his robberies. In his mind, the shooting was the victim's fault because that person had been reckless enough to risk his life for the money demanded of him by the robber.[4] These people have spent their entire lives exploiting other people, and so have developed a very sophisticated self-image through which they see themselves as victims of their environments and the real victims as people who "had it coming."

Combining this anger with a very selective conscience, these people have an uncanny ability to justify even the most heinous acts. I once had occasion to do counseling with a person convicted of murdering another man, and I listened as he described how he planned and carried out his crime. He felt that because this person had made sexual advances toward him, this excused his lying in wait days later and shooting the victim repeatedly with a rifle. Through this type of self-deception, criminals often spend their lifetimes violating, abusing, and killing other people, all the while justifying their reasons for doing it.

Volumes have been written regarding the true motives behind deviant criminal behavior. Causal factors contributing to crime have been identified as dysfunctional family relationships, genetic abnormalities, neurochemical imbalances, and adverse socioeconomic conditions. Samenow examines a number of these influences[5] while Ressler and Shachtman focus on underlying psychosexual drives unique to serial killers.[6]

Still, they and most other knowledgeable experts conclude that criminals commit violent acts against others primarily because of their ability to devalue human life. From the earliest years of their development, these societal deviants somehow fail to learn the appropriate human emotional responses toward others in the world around them. This fact gives an almost eerie credence to the biblical teaching that states, "The wicked go astray from the womb, they err from their birth, speaking lies" (Ps. 58.3).

Due to the lack of normal socialization processes, these people eventually come to maintain a strange sense of detachment from nearly all other people. Their value system is absent any meaningful regard for human life; and because of this, the act of taking a human life has no more significance for them than swatting a fly.

These are the kinds of societal mistakes that can beat an innocent person to death for no reason, then go drink beer with their buddies and laugh about how amusing it was to watch the victim die. They can commit any atrocity and experience absolutely no guilt or remorse. As these people continue to kill, they actually begin to enjoy the act of murder because it substantiates their perceived superiority over others.

This behavior was well illustrated at the trial of a gang member convicted of murdering a Fort Worth, Texas, police officer. The victim's brother, Dave, and I graduated from the police academy in 1977 and have maintained our friendship since. Dave shared with me how his brother's murderer reacted upon hearing the sentence. Showing no remorse whatsoever, this cop killer simply raised his arm in the Crips gang salute and proclaimed for those present in the courtroom, "Crips for life."

Perhaps one of the most insidious characteristics of many sociopaths is their unassuming physical appearance. They are often perceived by others as being genuinely charming people. This incredible ability to disguise their diabolic personalities with a charismatic veneer is crucial to the success of their sinister actions. Through this guise, the effective sociopath is able to con money from an unsuspecting elderly person, lure a young woman out of a club and into his car, or charm his way into the life of the woman soon to be his next murder victim.

Consider interviews with neighbors and acquaintances of murderers Gacy and Bundy. Incredibly, those interviewed consistently describe such heartless entities as "ordinary," often "likeable," even "outgoing" people. They stated that they would never have suspected that these killers could be "the kind of person to do such a thing."

I will always believe that my mother probably unknowingly came in contact with her murderer sometime prior to her death. His friendly face could very easily have been one of the many she encountered during her trips to the grocery store, the drugstore, the beauty shop, the shopping mall, or any number of other places she frequented. Until the moment he revealed his deadly plan, I believe she would never have imagined what his hideous intentions were. And by then, of course, her fate had already been sealed.

Finally, the antisocial personality disorder, as it is with other personality disorders (i.e., narcissistic personality, obsessive-compulsive personality, histrionic personality) is considered an "irreversible" condition.[7] These people characteristically do not respond to normal mental health therapies, so their emotional conditions are considered incurable for all intents and purposes.

In the context of their criminal activities, the implications of this fact for the rest of society is very serious. Psychopaths—rapists and murderers in particular—are considered by most experts to be incorrigible offenders who cannot be rehabilitated. Therefore, the only certain way of ensuring that society is kept safe from these people is to execute them or incarcerate them for life. Our liberal criminal justice system, with its "revolving door" prison policies, however, makes lifelong imprisonment very difficult.

As one anonymous law enforcement official stated, "In the criminal justice system, nothing means anything anymore. Life imprisonment doesn't mean life, death doesn't mean death, and twenty-five years means twelve and a half, or maybe even six." Therefore, the system continues to release these people time and time again, often after they have served only a fraction of their sentences. Thus, they continue preying, at will, upon anyone in society.

Though much of this is painfully apparent to me in retrospect, until the time of my mother's disappearance, I had little sense of just how drastically this type of individual could affect me personally. Certainly, my police experience in the streets of Fort Worth, Texas, and Lenexa, Kansas, in the 1970s had taught me much. You don't take anything for granted, you never turn your back on someone, and, with few exceptions, you don't trust anyone. I had worked enough burglaries, car thefts, DUIs (driving under the influence), assaults, robberies, and murders to know that there were a frightening number of dangerous people out there victimizing society.

My perspective at that time, though, had been relatively sterile and detached. I went back to normalcy at the end of my shift and tried not to think about the havoc wrought by the social refuse I kept sweeping off the streets. Suddenly, fifteen years later, I was getting my own painful education in the agony experienced by the victims of the same criminal actions that I had so casually tried to put out of my mind.

***

By the end of the first week following Mother's disappearance, I had already come to the conclusion that I would never see her alive again.

It was at this point that another terrible reality became evident to me—one that as a Christian I did not want to accept. This was the recognition that in an evil world, God often does not protect His own.

My mother was a believing Christian who had maintained a strong faith in God's power to impact her life. She had committed virtually all her problems—physical, emotional, and spiritual—to Him, trusting Him to solve them for her. How ironic it was that the plaque quoting Psalm 56:3—"In what time I am afraid, I will trust"—hung on the wall in the very room from which she had been abducted.

I was suddenly forced to accept that in her most desperate hour, as she likely faced death at the hands of a monster, He had not protected her from harm. Where was her God then when she needed Him?

Perhaps you have shared these same misgivings. You spend your lifetime naively believing, or at least hoping, that God will protect His own. You've heard the testimonies in church about all the good things He has done for other people. You've read about the miracles that people have experienced, sometimes even being saved from death itself.

So in this darkest hour of crisis, when you most need the assurance that God is with you, you find yourself wondering why He could meet their needs and not yours. You ask yourself, is your God this capricious master of the universe who favors one for some reason and not the other? How, you say, can He possibly stand by and watch as one of His own is violated, injured, tortured, or killed?

This seems to be one of the most tormenting questions for victims of criminal actions. I have heard many homicide survivors tearfully express how angry they are with God for allowing the loss of their loved one. They know He was watching as their son or daughter was murdered, and since He could have prevented it, they hold Him to be ultimately responsible for their loss. Logical or otherwise, this perspective is the dominant reality for most survivors.

I believe these misgivings represent a terrible paradox of faith to believers. One explanation is that God is only capable of so much. He cannot physically reach down from heaven and stop the course of evil in this world.[8] From this perspective, He is incapable of altering the course of earthly events playing themselves out for us on a daily basis. To believe this is to absolve God of responsibility in our loss;

but at the same time, we are effectively saying that He does not hold absolute control over this universe. If this is so, are we then not wasting our time committing our lives to such an impotent God?

The other perspective of faith holds that God remains the all-powerful Creator of the universe who can direct the course of every action on earth *if* He so chooses. To believe this, though, is to admit that He did not act on our behalf when He could have.

You may have rightfully asked yourself, *If He could part the Red Sea long enough for half a million Israelis to cross, could He not have given my daughter thirty seconds to get off the street before that gunfire started?* Perhaps you have tormented yourself with the knowledge that the same Christ who physically turned water into wine could not somehow direct a drunk driver into a guardrail instead of head-on into your husband's car.

Accepting my tenet of faith—that our God is still capable today of performing the same miracles He did thousands of years ago—is very painful in this context. We are now forced to confront the agonizing reality that He purposely stood by and watched as we, or someone we love, was humiliated, brutalized, or murdered. What does this say about His love for us, and how does this influence our obligation to Him in return?

On a cognitive level, we can attempt to justify these inconsistencies by reminding ourselves that our loss was a result of perverted choices exercised by evil people. We try to respect the fact that after all these years, God still allows our right to self-determination in spite of its devastating consequences.

Nevertheless, on an emotional plane, we can only see the injustice of it all. We are now jealous of those instances where He acted miraculously to save another person, but refused to do so for our loved one or us. We resent the fact that He spared someone else from violence, while allowing our loved one to be destroyed.

What, then, is His formula for justice? What criteria do we have to meet to be saved by Him from destruction?

Even if it were somehow possible for us to objectively accept these disparities, our pain, anguish, and grief at the time of our loss blind us to objectivity. We are left only with the aching desire to return to a life that was untouched by evil, a life in which an unquestioned faith in God's power still directed our existence.

***

Near the end of the second week after Mother's disappearance, I knew that it was only a matter of time before I would collapse under the weight of my emotional ordeal. I couldn't stand the unending uncertainty. When my sister and I finally decided we had to do something, we both made airline reservations for Wichita to sort out firsthand what we were facing. Any reality, no matter how horrible, was better than succumbing to the slow death we were both experiencing at that time.

I contemplated my terrible circumstances and all the doubts that threatened everything I had believed for a lifetime as I flew back to Kansas, unaware that my worst nightmare was about to become reality within the next forty-eight hours.

CHAPTER 3

THE ULTIMATE MADNESS

My heart is in anguish within me, the terrors
of death have fallen upon me.
Fear and trembling come upon me, and horror overwhelms me.

—Psalms 55:4–5

Mother's body was discovered the morning after we arrived in Wichita. We learned later that she had been dead since the night she disappeared. The cause of death would be determined to be suffocation resulting from strangulation by ligature.

Laurel; her husband, Rob; and I were with Sam, the chief investigator, going through Mother's safe deposit box early that morning when Sam's beeper went off. I heard the dispatcher tell him to call immediately because it was an emergency.

After Sam had returned the call and I questioned him about it, he quickly told us that it had nothing to do with our case. He is the kind of person who is too honest to be a convincing liar, so I suspected that someone had probably found Mother's body. Still, I kept this thought to myself while we struggled through the emotional ordeal of going through her personal effects.

As Laurel, Rob, and I walked into the sheriff's office later that morning, Sam's face said it all. He immediately took Rob and me into an interrogation room and told us that the body of an older, white female had been discovered in the extreme northern part of Sedgwick County, almost at the Harvey County line. Sam said that the forensics people were still working the scene and did not yet have positive identification.

My palms were sweating. I had a hard time catching my breath, and I felt almost nauseous when he said that they would need me to identify the body. At that point, all the uncertainty, frustration, fear, and dread of the last two weeks surfaced. I had endured what seemed like a lifetime of agony, not knowing if my mother was dead, yet certain in my own mind that she was. I had prayed repeatedly that if she had been killed, we could at least find her body and put that terrible question to rest. I had tormented myself throughout that time over what fate she had suffered and who had been responsible for it. I had tried in every way possible to prepare myself for this moment, but once it arrived, I couldn't face it. How could I bear the prospect of viewing the result of murder at the hands of the devil and two weeks' exposure to the elements?

For one of the few times in my life, I refused to accept a responsibility that had been laid solely at my feet. Fighting to control my anger and embarrassment, I told him that I couldn't do what had to be done—that he would just have to find someone else.

Later that day, my mother's brother, Gary, agreed to make the identification; but Sam told us it could be well into the evening before they would be ready for that. There was nothing else we could do but wait. We whiled away the rest of the day at the house of my best friend's parents, Carl and Betty, trying to make polite conversation but consumed with anxiety.

We suffered through the local newscasts describing how "the body of an unidentified older woman had been discovered north of town." We listened to speculation on whether this was "connected to the case of Dolores Davis, who has been missing now for two weeks." We were incensed when one local news anchor erroneously stated that he had been informed by a "source close to the investigation that the woman's throat had been cut."

Since Laurel was seven months pregnant, I was very concerned about what effect this trauma would have on her. Eventually, we settled into an evening routine where we all sat in silence, once again waiting for a call we dreaded.

It was close to midnight when the investigators finally requested that my uncle meet them downtown. By the time I reached the sheriff's office, my uncle and the detectives had already completed the process. I don't think I even said anything; I just looked at Gary, and he said, "We're 99.9 percent sure it was your mother." They were going to have to rely on dental records for total confirmation, but we were all forced to accept the terrible reality that we had feared for two endless weeks.

I cannot recall a lower point in my life than that instant represented. At that moment, my worst horror became reality. There would be no more denial, no more doubt. Fate had just dealt me one of the worst possible hands that anyone could be forced to play. Everything I had ever believed, experienced, or valued for a lifetime was altered in an instant.

The formerly abstract concept of a devil who orchestrated evil in this world at the expense of others had suddenly taken on an entirely new meaning. Evil incarnate had just robbed me of someone I had loved and depended on for thirty-nine years. The irrational actions of one malevolent ego had resulted in the loss of a mother, a sister, an aunt, a grandmother, and a friend to countless people. One heartless animal, devoid of all human feelings, had coldly calculated, executed, and savored the act of killing an innocent person for reasons known only to him and God. One psychopath's efforts to destroy a stranger who vicariously represented his "enemy" had set in motion a chain reaction of grief and misery that would impact innumerable lives for years to come.

The thought of a sovereign, loving God who controlled the universe had never been farther from my mind.

***

For most of us who are survivors of violence, this moment of acceptance represents the point at which the most intense emotional and spiritual battles begin. We can no longer avoid the horrible truth that we have permanently lost something irreplaceable. Our self-image is transformed as we begin to see ourselves as people whose lives have forever been stigmatized by the actions of uncompromising evil. Our sense of security is altered as we recognize, just as Job did, that this world truly is a violent place. Our trust in God may be shaken as we wonder why He could have allowed such a thing to happen.

I believe that in accepting this new reality, we actually terminate a perspective of life based upon one set of values, and begin establishing another perspective of life built upon a new set of assumptions about this world and our God.

If we are the victims ourselves, we begin the arduous process of trying to accept the fact that we have been violated in the most personal way, whether physically or emotionally. If we survive someone who has been killed, we wonder how we will be able to exist without that precious loved one. How, we wonder, will we ever fill that enormous void? We can't deny the fact that this madness has cheated us immeasurably, that our loss is entirely in vain, and we experience intense bitterness and anger as a result.

Almost as quickly as this sense of anger and betrayal has set in, we begin mounting a campaign to assign responsibility to someone or something for our circumstances. There must be some reason for this chaos, and that reason must be attributable to someone, we conclude. We, or someone we care for, has been aggrieved in the worst possible way. We feel compelled to ask who is to blame: what could have prevented the loss?

As survivors, we seem to share a need to blame ourselves as a part of this process. Could we have done something differently to avoid placing ourselves in harm's way? What might we have done to prevent our loved one's death or injury? Surely, there must have been a way to avoid this.

Ironically, these self-recriminations represent the beginning of a re-victimization process in which survivors are often victimized repeatedly in a number of other social contexts.

This re-victimization is sometimes initially seen in the survivors' interaction with law enforcement authorities. Despite most police officers' good intentions, they become hardened by years of exposure to society at its worst. Daily encounters with violence, death, and unspeakable acts cause many police officers to avoid dealing with their feelings. To do otherwise can be overwhelming for them, so they often try to disguise their real emotions through emotional withdrawal, black humor, and other evasive behaviors. This serves as their defense mechanism.

As a result, they sometimes appear calloused and uncaring when working with victims of crime. This is not intentional, but is a result of this defense mechanism responding to intolerable circumstances. Investigators' onslaught of questions regarding specifics of the offense may seem accusatory and judgmental at times to an emotionally distraught victim or family member.

From the investigators' perspective, however, they are simply attempting to obtain the facts and identify the perpetrator. They are trained to be suspicious of everyone, even the survivors of victims. This is particularly true in homicides, because statistically, most people are murdered by family members or friends. Therefore, most police officers' ability to adequately address the emotional needs of grieving victims is often absent.

For this reason, victims advocate services can play a crucial role. Many law enforcement agencies today are utilizing the services of these personnel to benefit the bereaved. Victims' advocates are trained to respond immediately to the scene of a crime. They are skilled in focusing specifically on the needs of the victim by providing nonjudgmental emotional support. They offer assistance with such tasks as contacting family, friends, and clergy or other activities that victims may be too distraught at the time to perform.

The Orange County (FL) Sheriff's Office represents a bellwether example of one proactive law enforcement agency that has been successfully utilizing victim advocate services for several years. Still, as beneficial as most of these programs have proven to be within their limited application, they have yet to be implemented across the board within the justice system, as I believe they ultimately must be.

Continued re-victimization is readily apparent in the manner in which the news media often dehumanize the events surrounding violent crime, particularly murders. Some reporters swarm around surviving family like starving buzzards, shoving microphones in the faces of distraught family members asking such inane questions as, "How do you feel about this?" and "Were you shocked to hear the news?" Survivors rightfully become irate when these unscrupulous newspeople capitalize on their misery for the sake of promoting sales copy or increasing television ratings. It is no wonder victims quickly come to feel exploited as a result of their loss.

Probably the most repugnant example of the media exploiting victims occurred during the notorious O.J. Simpson trial of 1995. The American public was literally besieged with constant coverage of every possible bit of trivia surrounding this trial—the color of Johnnie Cochran's tie, Marcia Clark's latest hairdo, the background of every witness. For those truly hungering for sensationalism, the defendant's friend, Al Cowlings, even established a telephone hotline to provide callers (at their own expense, of course) with his "unbiased" account of trial proceedings.

While the public was overwhelmed with this media assault, how much was written about the grief consuming the lives of the victims' families? Did anyone seem to care that the two victims who died hideous deaths were almost immediately forgotten in this media feeding frenzy? Was anyone concerned with the desperation Ronald Goldman's parents endured because of his senseless death? Did anyone write about how Nicole Brown Simpson's family coped with their loss? Were these bereaved family members interviewed about how intolerable it must have been for them to watch the defendant roll his eyes and joke with his lawyers during the trial proceedings? I saw little coverage of these legitimate human interest stories.

Even friends may contribute to this re-victimization process by unknowingly implying that survivors bear some degree of responsibility for their loss. A battery victim may be questioned by well-meaning friends as to why she was alone in that situation. The victim of an armed robber may be asked by friends why he was out so late that night. Survivors of homicide victims are invariably asked about the circumstances surrounding the murder. What remain unsaid are their thoughts that perhaps the victim might have in some way avoided the circumstances that resulted in their death.

In reality, what difference do the actions of the victim make? If a woman walks topless down the street, it is stupid, immoral, and usually illegal; but does that give another the right to violate her? If a man withdraws a thousand dollars at 3:00 a.m. from an automated bank machine in a seedy part of town, he may be guilty of gross negligence, but does that justify a sociopath beating him half to death?

People associated with survivors sometimes appear compelled to address these events with a cause-and-effect logic. I believe they may go to great lengths to explain this violence to themselves in terms of the victim's responsibility for his/her circumstances. It represents the safest course of action for them.

"If she hadn't been involved with those people..."

"If he hadn't been in that place..."

"If she had been more careful..."

These are all ways of saying that the victim was in some measure at fault. In this manner, they can distance themselves from the possibility that they could ever become victims themselves.

As long as they believe that they can avoid being victimized by doing the sensible things, associating with the right people, and using good judgment, then they can deceive themselves into believing that they are immune from the epidemic of violence surrounding everyone. Using this "If only they'd..." logic may provide them with some peace of mind, but it has instilled a tremendous sense of guilt in many victims.

This is why murders like my mother's are so threatening. This simplistic cause-and-effect logic doesn't apply. The fact that a kind, unassuming lady—with no known enemies and guilty of absolutely nothing in relation to her death—was strangled in her own home for no rational motive, flies in the face of this naive logic. What part did she play in her death? What did she do to deserve murder at the hands of a stranger? How can these incidents be explained?

The fact is that they can't be explained logically. The truth is that evil runs rampant in this world, that truly vicious people wait anxiously to prey on innocent victims, that everyone is a potential victim, and that anyone may be killed at any time for no conceivable reason. This lack of logic, however, is too threatening for most people to accept, so they generally choose to rationalize events.

Nowhere is the surviving family members' sense of re-victimization more obvious than in the legal proceedings surrounding a homicide trial. Not legally recognized as victims in most states, those surviving the victim represent what I believe to be *invisible victims* or *forgotten casualties*—those unnoticed survivors of violence in our society. Even the deceased, in legal terms, is not actually represented in court. Strictly speaking, prosecution of a homicide case involves the state versus the defendant. The victim is simply the means by which the state tries a defendant for a crime.

This is well illustrated in the case of my friends Jim and Carol, whose son, Jamie, was brutally murdered. During the course of the trial, Jim was pressing the district attorney for additional information regarding his son's case. The prosecutor callously reminded Jim that the prosecution did not represent their son but, in fact, represented the State of Michigan. From the perspective of that prosecutor, it should have been obvious that Jamie was simply the means to the State's legal end.

The irony of this case is that Jim and Carol's son had, in fact, been an attorney himself. This family had staunchly believed in the sanctity of our legal system. Their exposure to the practices of "justice" on behalf of their son, however, have since changed their feelings in this respect.

This type of legal climate establishes a terribly dehumanizing atmosphere for too many grieving family members. Survivors' perception that their loved ones have been lost in the legal "shuffle" is often absolutely correct.

In many states today, survivors can still be banned from the courtroom during the trial. A simple objection from the defense that such would be "prejudicial to the jury" can result in their being eliminated from the whole trial process. Even in states like Florida, where victims are guaranteed this right, it can be easily circumvented by a shrewd defense attorney. If the family of the victim "disturbs" the trial in any way, including the display of any emotion at all, they are quickly removed from the courtroom.

A favorite trick of devious defense lawyers is to subpoena a victim's relative, with no intention of calling her to the witness stand. This ensures that the family member will be excluded from nearly all of the trial proceedings because witnesses can have no part in the court events except for their own testimony.

Conversely, the criminal is well insulated from the ordeals of the court proceedings. Often the accused is unable or unwilling to secure his own defense, so he is represented by a public defender at no cost to him. Defense attorneys, often suspecting their clients' guilt, try to shift the guilt of their clients to phantom suspects whom they create to place doubt in the minds of jury members.

While defense attorneys can wreak havoc with witnesses and victims on the stand, they nearly always advise their clients not to testify. This is because they know that a good prosecutor would rip their client's story to pieces and reveal their guilt. Thus, their legal charade can focus on impugning the innocent, while the guilty cower beneath the skirts of Lady Justice.

Finally, many professing Christians unwittingly contribute to the re-victimization of survivors by reminding them that they are obligated to forgive the ones responsible for their loss. As a result of this pressure, many survivors experience tremendous guilt unnecessarily. They feel they should forgive, and yet know in their hearts that forgiveness is years away, if ever attainable.

Obviously, a fundamental precept of Christianity is the practice of forgiveness. Christ embodied this attribute throughout His life on earth. He even asked the forgiveness of God for those who brutally nailed him to the cross. No more powerful example of unqualified forgiveness can be found anywhere in man's history.

However, I must raise the question as to whether it was possible for even God to grant this request of His own dying Son. Was God's forgiveness attainable for those who put His Son to death, if those who took part in it did not genuinely seek God's forgiveness?

As a Christian, I see God paradoxically as both supremely just and equally forgiving. However, I believe that if each of us does not sincerely seek His forgiveness prior to death, we will be subject to His righteous condemnation of our imperfect lives. Therefore, I am not certain that even God Himself can extend forgiveness if it is not sincerely requested of Him by the criminal offender.

Countless criminals claim to experience a Christian conversion sometime subsequent to their arrest. This is what embittered and resentful survivors refer to as finding their "jailhouse Jesus." Few of these people, however, approach their victims or their victims' families to ask forgiveness for their crimes and demonstrate genuine repentance for their actions. Therefore, I question whether we, representing the survivor community, need allow ourselves to be re-victimized over the issue of forgiving our aggressors until such time as we are asked to extend it.

CHAPTER 4

STARING INTO THE
ABYSS OF LOSS

As for man, his days are like grass; he flourishes like
a flower of the field; for the wind passes over it, and
it is gone, and its place knows it no more.

—Psalms 103:15–16

As we all know, the death of any loved one represents a tremendous change in the lives of those left behind. People sometimes spend years learning how to readjust to a world in which that loved one is no longer a part. For most people, the funeral represents the first step in driving home the reality that this person is permanently gone from their lives.

Most funeral services today involve some opportunity for survivors to view the body of the deceased, either at a viewing prior to the service or at some point during the actual funeral. This is an extension of the ancient Jewish rite of sitting shiva. This offered family and friends a period of time for sitting with the body of the deceased and formally grieving, thus beginning the readjustment process in their loss.

This, however, was not possible in our case because of the time frame between Mother's death and the discovery of her body.

We therefore had no opportunity to make that critical emotional connection confirming the reality of loss, which is available only when one can actually see the person in death. I discovered months later that lack of this visual confirmation offers a type of emotional loophole through which the subconscious mind may deny reality of the other's death.

Nevertheless, at the time, Laurel and I had done our best under the terrible pressures of the preceding week to make Mother's funeral a fitting testament to her life.

We knew in advance that the police would be videotaping the service. They had explained beforehand that sometimes in these "motiveless" murders, the perpetrator will actually attend the funeral services. Later research on my part confirmed that serial killers do sometimes attend the funeral as a way of relishing their accomplishment and savoring their victory over society. Therefore, we tried to take this distraction in stride, hoping to give the police every possible advantage in solving this case.

The service itself would probably be considered beautiful by others more detached than I was. Mother had stated in her will that since she had few friends, a small and very simple service would be appropriate. Laurel and I were to do nothing elaborate and, above all, we were to keep it simple. As was typical of Mother's nature, she had vastly underestimated her worth in the eyes of others. Well over one hundred people, including a number of folks from her 1945 high school graduating class, packed the funeral parlor that unusually mild Wichita afternoon of February 9.

Per her request, we included several of her favorite songs, such as "Softly and Tenderly," "Danny Boy," and "The Day He Wore My Crown." Our mother had a studio-quality voice to rival Patsy Cline's, and since music had always been a big part of her life, we wanted the service to reflect that.

Adding to the beauty of the service was the rainbow of color provided by the floral arrangements that decorated the parlor and her coffin. I felt this was fitting, because she had always loved flowers so much when she was alive.

The eulogies provided by our pastor and her friends and family were most appropriate and greatly moving. In all, I believe the atmosphere was one that provided the best possible opportunity, under the circumstances, for all of us to pay her our final respects.

Nevertheless, I felt somehow alienated from everything around me because I was not allowed a normal grief. While I ached with a pain that I had experienced only once before, with the death of my father thirteen years earlier, the predominant emotion crowding out my anguish was rage.

I sat with tears welling up, refusing to allow them escape, as I pondered the significance of this huge crowd and listened to the wonderful words attesting to my mother's life. All the while, my thoughts centered on exacting revenge against the human monstrosity that was responsible for all of this grief.

As Mother's cousin read "Forever Hope," I kept trying to envision what the murderer looked like, how old he was, or whether he could really be out there in attendance. Even as our pastor spoke of what a kind and forgiving person she had been, I kept thinking that all I wanted at that moment was to kill her murderer. Many people wept as a friend read Temple Bailey's "Parable of Motherhood," and I could only clench my jaw in fury.

Although I am not proud of it, had I come face-to-face with her murderer that day, I have absolutely no doubt that I would have killed him. I recognize now that had I somehow been able to get hold of him in that crowd, I would have beaten him to death with my own hands. For that was the only time in my life I was consumed with a primal rage strong enough to drive me to commit the ultimate sin in the presence of one hundred witnesses.

So as the service concluded with the playing of "Amazing Grace," and as everyone slowly filed past her closed casket, I sat there silently, displaying no outward signs of emotion. Internally, a battle was raging between my anger and my sorrow, and I think anger prevailed because it was less evident to others and therefore less threatening to me. I was afraid that if I gave in to my overwhelming grief of the moment, I would probably drown in my own tears.

Being the final person to pay my respects at her coldly sealed coffin, I choked back the tidal wave of despair and loneliness washing over me and desperately focused on my rage to help me survive the rest of the day.

I spent my last evening in Wichita before returning to Orlando, struggling to fathom the full impact of this last hideous week. Throughout that night, I searched for the significance of the fact that a young boy walking his dog had just "happened" upon Mother's body, the very day after we had arrived. In my mind, it had been no coincidence that the call regarding this event had come at the exact time we had been with Sam in the bank vault. I had little doubt that my prayer for the discovery of her body—with all the horror it represented—had been answered at that exact moment.

Still, this brought me no comfort. Why couldn't my prayer that she be found alive and well have been answered instead? Why hadn't my prayers for the identification of her murderer and the satisfaction of justice been answered? Why was any of this nightmare occurring in the first place?

I later discovered that this particular answer to prayer represented the last response I would receive for many months to come. Unknowingly, I had already entered one of the loneliest and most desperate periods of my life.

***

Many times, the ash of loneliness associated with the death of a loved one doesn't settle completely until long after the funeral service. Immediately after any death, there is the inevitable flurry of activity needed to plan the service, contact extended family and out-of-state friends, notify insurance companies, and handle a myriad other details and loose ends. Often, such stresses are shared by friends, church members, and others who help by making funeral arrangements, bringing in food, assisting with young children, and providing emotional and prayer support. There is such nonstop activity throughout this time that people have little opportunity to ponder the full implications of their loss.

Then ultimately comes the still silence following the funeral. Nothing else is to be done, little remains to be said, friends and family resume their normal routines, and those left behind begin the arduous task of facing the reality of life absent of a much-loved and much-needed person.

In addition to these always-painful adjustments, those surviving a homicide victim are faced with additional adversities. For one, the pressures associated with police investigations or criminal trials continue, sometimes long after the funeral. While those bereaved by other circumstances are able to begin the process of accepting a new reality for their lives at this point, the family of a homicide victim is forced to continue dealing with these stressful legal procedures. They may be required to furnish more statements, provide additional information about the victim, appear in court to testify, or address questions from the news media. This not only ensures that old wounds continue to fester, but it also prohibits the quiet personal time required to begin accepting all the realities of their loss.

Their unending search to make sense of their loss remains their daily tormentor. They realize that they will face the remainder of their lives contemplating the elusive *why*'s responsible for their fate; and this prospect seems insufferable. Related issues—their questions surrounding the death, their doubts of faith, their concept of right and wrong, their perspective of justice and injustice—all complicate their reconstruction process. Unfortunately, their continued sojourn down the road of unattainable answers often leads to nothing but more pain and frustration.

When confronted with profound questions like the reasons behind violent death, many explanations have been offered over the years. One school of thought implies that God sometimes takes a person by way of these circumstances because He had something better in mind (in an eternal context) for him.[1]

If this is so, then the cynic in me feels we must indeed serve a cruel master if He allows a teenage girl to be tortured and killed as her shortcut to heaven. If our God permits the father of two small children to be murdered during an armed robbery because He has some special assignment for him in heaven, then He is not the loving God of all mercy I was raised to worship. I am afraid such a perspective of profound tragedy neither affords me comfort in my loss nor strengthens my faith in my time of need.

I believe the age-old adage that "it was God's will" is often used by those who cannot think of any other answer for madness of this order. While it may provide them with some false sense of security to believe that every event in this universe is directly controlled by God's hand, it denies reality. Even worse, it also serves to undermine the survivor's already-tenuous faith in His goodness.

Is a husband supposed to find solace because God's will somehow involved a pair of savage psychopaths robbing his wife, beating her to unconsciousness, then running over her with her car while her children watched? Is the mother of a young girl, raped and killed by a group of crazed gang members, going to feel better because her daughter's death was in some way part of God's greater plan for the universe?

The ever-escalating violence in our world should leave little doubt that while God does have an ultimate, eternal plan for this world and each of us in it, His involvement in controlling our every action on a day-to-day basis is very limited. It is my firm conviction that those believing otherwise are extremely naive.

It has also been offered by some writers that we should view such atrocities from a more positive perspective. This school of thought suggests that as a result of our having experienced tragedy, we will be better people in the long run, because suffering produces a quality of character in us not available under normal circumstances.

Victor Frankl graphically describes his own experiences in the hideous World War II Nazi concentration camp of Auschwitz. Conditions there were so horrible that only one prisoner in twenty survived. Yet in the midst of such misery he came to understand that these very circumstances had unleashed an element of character in him otherwise unattainable. He had determined that he would put these terrible experiences to use in his life in a positive way, and he was able to survive as a result, while most of those around him gave up and died.[2]

Perhaps I speak for many survivors when I say that if these ordeals are the only way that I can learn some of life's most profound lessons, and become a better Christian as a result, I would like to pass on this aspect of my education. The suffering experienced in the six-month convalescence of a battery victim, the emotional turmoil following a rape victim throughout her life, or the mental agony of the parents of a murdered child may somehow serve to develop some hidden aspects of their character; but they would probably agree with me that the price to be paid in acquiring these greater personal insights is far higher than most of us would willingly pay.

Nearly all grief processes are characterized by regret. A person berates himself for not having called the victim more often, for having said something harsh in a heated moment, or for such things as having forgotten a birthday or other significant events.

While these self-recriminations are common with any loss, they are significantly magnified when the deceased was the victim of violence. For instance, my sister Laurel still experiences guilt because of a heated argument she and Mother had near the end of our final Christmas visit.

Survivors commonly generate such strong feelings of guilt that they may spend years working through them. For some perverse reason, surviving family members feel compelled to twist the emotional knife of guilt as often as possible, perhaps subconsciously resorting to this as penance for their perceived culpability in the loss. I believe this stems from a previously described illogical, but emotionally powerful, conviction that they somehow could have or should have done something to prevent the other's death.

My emotional component has reminded my logical self uncountable times that I should have been there to stop the murder of my mother. In reality, of course, I could have nothing done from 1,500 miles away, even if I had somehow known exactly what was about to happen. Still, I sometimes lie awake at night, blaming myself for all that I didn't do for my mother in her time of desperate need. I torture myself imagining that she probably cried out my name in the vain hope that I could somehow prevent the inevitable.

Logic again offers little solace to us who have lost others to violence, because all we see is the many "what if's" and "if only's" that torment our lives as we mentally replay our horror over and over for years.

As an extension of this guilt, many survivors are tortured by memories of happier times with the deceased. At some point in a normal grieving process, these pleasant memories become a source of inspiration and solace for family members. But this process generally takes much longer for those affected by violent death. This is a result of our knowledge that our good times with a loved one were cut arbitrarily and brutally short through the malevolent actions of another. We can never forget that what should be present reality is now past memory for no justifiable reason.

A mother weeps every time she goes in to clean her daughter's room, finally locking the door and resolving never to go back in. Parents cry every time they look at their son's wedding picture, which now mocks them with the question, "Remember how good life once was?" As a father fights insomnia, the mental image of that once-proud moment when his son caught his first touchdown pass now serves as his nightly tormentor. To this day, I avoid my mother's pictures spread throughout our house, because they still cause for me more pain than peace.

The power of a survivor's mental image of the lost one at this emotionally susceptible time should not be underestimated. Nearly every survivor with whom I have associated has mentioned being strongly impacted by some haunting reminder of a loved one.

This may involve imagining that they have actually felt the presence of that person in their home. It may consist of a recurrent, detailed visualization of that person's face. Often, it hangs in the mind as the sound of the other's voice.

I can still hear my mother's voice as she spoke with me during that last visit; I hear her as she told my son and my daughter how much they had grown; and I can recall distinctly how she sounded when she answered her telephone at work. The startling reality of these images may perhaps be psychologically analogous to the phenomenon of phantom physical pains experienced by those who have lost a limb.

Some of the most arduous times for the survivors of violence can be holidays and special occasions, especially within the first year of loss. My association with support groups has confirmed my experience that many of these people dread the arrival of the deceased's birthday, Father's or Mother's Day, or a wedding anniversary. Mother's Day of 1991 was almost unbearable for me, as it intensified the tremendous depression I was already struggling to overcome. Of course, the special holidays of Christmas and Thanksgiving are ruined for the family experiencing the loss. They represent ordeals to be endured, painful reminders of what might have been, rather than the happy and festive occasions they are supposed to be. I refused to celebrate either of these holidays that first year because I certainly did not feel thankful, and all the promises of Christmas were empty and meaningless to me.

Probably the most loathsome day of the calendar for any victim or survivor is the anniversary of the violence. Many survivors experience a terrible kind of dread, often weeks in advance, as the anniversary of the most horrible day of their lives inevitably approaches. Friends and family need to be acutely aware that this is a period of extreme duress for these individuals, some of whom may even become suicidal.

Friends and family should, therefore, be subtly available and quietly supportive in an effort to ease this pain as much as possible. A change of physical environment might be helpful. Such a diversion—a movie, a walk through the park, a sporting event—can serve to temporarily ease the terrible emotional burden that can become overwhelming at times. Such strategies are especially important near the significant dates such as birthdays, anniversaries, and holidays.

Above all, providing survivors the opportunity to express their feelings is imperative. Such strong negative emotions will probably be threatening to the listener. Survivors may demonstrate intense feelings of rage—toward the world, their offenders, or even the listener. They may even exhibit seemingly inappropriate emotional reactions such as hysterical laughing or apparent serenity. Still, a true friend will be willing to endure this discomfort for the sake of aiding the bereaved's emotional well-being. Even if survivors choose not to express themselves, they will greatly appreciate the listener's willingness to hear them out rather than acting as if their pain did not exist.

Perhaps most critical in providing assistance is the need for friends to remind the bereaved that what occurred was not the fault of the victim. Reinforcing the fact that cruelty and evil, not the victim, are responsible for what occurred, can be very reassuring to a guilt-ridden survivor. Supporting them by verbalizing that what happened was terribly unfair, that you share their pain, and that you will always remain their friend may be the only solace they receive during these desperate and lonely times.

The last words of support that these folks want to hear, however, is "I understand" or "It will be all right." Unless those listening are themselves survivors, they certainly have no inkling of what empathetic understanding in these circumstances means. To be told that everything will be "all right" is a denial of the victim's entire life experience at that point. They know full well that their lives will never again be the same, so for them, it can't ever be all right again.

In these vulnerable times, the survivor will respond much more favorably to an emotional or physical pat on the back, a reminder that they matter, or just a friendly smile and a willing presence.

Obviously, individuals respond differently to the same set of circumstances, and each of us grieves in a unique manner. Still, I have found in working with other survivors that men experience a grief process that is distinctly different from women, and that children likewise go through a grief process that is considerably different from that of adults. An understanding of the grief unique to violence victims can serve to reduce the inevitably great stress levels created under these circumstances.

Most males who have lost someone to violence will demonstrate tremendous amounts of rage throughout the grief cycle. Perhaps this is a result of our socialization process that discourages men from expressing sorrow but makes great allowances for them to act out angry feelings.

Repeatedly, I have heard men in survivors' groups express their grief in terms of how angry they are, and what they would do with the perpetrator if they could. Their graphic comments would offend the sensitivities of most people who have not experienced such loss. For those of us who have, though, we generally nod in silent agreement that these recriminations are entirely justified from our emotional standpoint.

I believe women also experience tremendous rage in their loss, but may have a harder time expressing their anger and wishful acts of retribution. While some women do readily express this rage, most of those I know evidence a grief that is apparent as intense sorrow. They are more effective than men in verbalizing their terrible sense of loss and sorrow and, unlike men, aren't afraid to express these feelings through crying or weeping in the presence of others. Again, this may stem from the socialization process that affords women this alternative more easily than men. Whatever the underlying source, these marked differences set up the potential for significant conflict between surviving husband and wife.

Early in my involvement with other survivors, my friends Joe and Jean exemplified these differences in the grieving process. Their thirty-year-old son, Joey, had been kidnapped by three youths, stuffed into the trunk of his own car, driven out near Walt Disney World, and shot in the back of the head.

Jean stated that Joe rarely discussed his feelings with her. She maintained that if he talked at all, it centered around his desire to ensure accountability for the ones responsible for their son's death. As a result, she sometimes felt isolated from the person whose support she most needed.

Their conversations in group revealed that his emotional perspective differed considerably from hers. Like Jean, he was also overwhelmed with grief, but expressing that sorrow was too difficult for him. He felt that he had to remain strong to assist her in her grief. Therefore, his focus at the time was primarily on bringing their son's killers to justice. Once they began sharing these feelings, they were able to build a bridge of understanding between their differences.

Add to this divergent husband-wife emotional equation the impact that such a loss has on children, and it becomes evident why the family of a homicide victim is often at great risk. It is my contention that children are amazingly resilient and can often handle emotional ordeals better than adults. Still, anyone who endures violent trauma will experience acute stress throughout the grief process, and children are no exception. The issue, then, is how it manifests itself within the family synergy.

My impression is that children tend to internalize their loss under these circumstances more so than do adults. While most men openly express their anger and women often evidence their sorrow, children often find a way of incorporating their loss into their daily lives without displaying many of the anticipated emotional reactions. Probably contributing to this is the fact that children have had little previous experience dealing with loss. Therefore, they have no role model by which they can determine what "acceptable" grief behavior is for them.

Perhaps the only positive result of the Oklahoma City bombing is that our society has been forced to confront the issue of children's death and grief. Hopefully, as an outcome of this tragedy, we will now do a better job of addressing the grieving process unique to children.

Our then-fourteen-year-old daughter, Amy, and eleven-year-old son, Jason, both demonstrated few outward emotions after the death of their grandmother. I therefore often wondered if they understood the full implications of their loss. Certainly, they had both attended the funeral and knew of the circumstances surrounding her death. Still, I saw none of the anger, bitterness, sorrow, regret, and guilt in their lives that I was battling constantly.

In later survivors' meetings, when they each expressed how the loss had impacted them, I came to the conclusion that their loss had been profound and their grief intense. Still, they had somehow been successful in accepting the undeniable and beginning the reconstruction process in their lives. Many times, after, in the depths of my unbearable depression and despair, I found myself wishing I could have adapted as well as they had, and wondering why I couldn't.

All too often, surviving husbands, wives, and children receive little, if any, support from friends, and no external assistance from group or individual counseling resources. This being the case, these differences in the grieving process become more pronounced and destructive, to the point that I suspect a disproportionate number of marriages end in divorce. A better understanding of this phenomenon and its impact on each family member, by the mental health community and friends and family of survivors, is essential if the likelihood of family destruction subsequent to violence is to be reduced in the future.

Additionally, I believe it is crucial that every function within our criminal justice system develop extensive victim support systems. Using victims advocate services as a model, each "link" in the criminal justice "chain" must begin instituting policies and services designed specifically to aid victims and family members as they make their way through the criminal justice maze.

Those involved in this process should include not only law enforcement personnel but also representatives from medical examiners' offices, court personnel, trial lawyer associations, and even representatives of the news media. Through the creation of such a support network, all personnel associated with the justice system will obtain a better understanding of how to demonstrate greater sensitivity in working with victims and their families. In return, most survivors' perception that the system is cruel and ineffective can be partially dispelled.

CHAPTER 5

THE INSATIABLE HUNGER FOR REVENGE

When a man causes a disfigurement in his neighbor,
as he has done it shall be done to him,
fracture for fracture, eye for eye, tooth for tooth.

—Leviticus 24:19–20

If love is the strongest of all emotions, being a homicide survivor tells me that hatred and the desire for revenge is a close second. I can think of few other circumstances that play more heavily upon the emotion of anger than victimization by a criminal act.

In those months following Mother's funeral, my anger and rage became well honed and fine-tuned to the point that most of my existence was focused on getting revenge against the human devil that had ruined my world.

Like so many other survivors, I slowly yielded to my resentment toward God for allowing Mother's murderer to get away with his atrocities. I found it easy to generalize my anger at both God and our worldly state of affairs as I pondered the magnitude of violence that exists unpunished today. I felt betrayed by God because He allowed so many of these outrages to go unpunished. As I thought of my own misery and that of those in similar circumstances, I could not understand how He could just sit back while societal beasts destroyed the lives of so many, and were not forced to answer for their evil.

This anger eventually became my constant companion. It was with me every morning when I woke up, and invariably intensified throughout the course of the day. My impatience in traffic was at a historic and dangerously high level. I often left survivor group meetings infuriated at the suffering I had witnessed. I usually had to leave the room at home if a television story detailing violence came on, because I was afraid my rage would boil over and I might explode.

Often, when the frustrations of the day accumulated to the point of overload, I lashed out at whoever (or whatever) was around. Unfortunately, the targets of these harangues and heated outbursts often proved to be my family. Even though they generally knew they were not the real cause of these explosions, eventually, my self-defeating behavior began to take its toll. They routinely steered a wide swath around me out of self-defense, which only served to magnify my growing sense of isolation.

I recognized that this internal anger was a bomb waiting to go off. I think I wanted so badly for someone to pay for what happened to my mother that I subconsciously projected my rage onto anyone who happened to get in my way. Not being oblivious to the danger, I prayed repeatedly for release from this burden.

Still, nothing seemed to change. No matter how hard I tried, or how many prayers I offered, the results in my life indicated that these petitions were nothing but empty words falling on deaf ears. I knew in my mind that with the right set of circumstances on the wrong given day, I might easily do something I would long regret.

One of the few strategies that helped me manage my anger was to plot ways that I could apprehend my mother's killer. I envisioned in great detail what I would do with him if I did. I could visualize exactly how I would get him to tell me *why* and *how* he had killed her. Determining the motives for his actions was almost as important as ensuring that he answered to me for taking my mother's life.

So powerful were these emotions that my pulse increased and my muscles tensed even as I imagined such an encounter. At one point, I became so enraged that I slammed my fist through a 3/8-inch-thick oak panel in our bedroom door. Unfortunately, this makeshift anger management technique was good only while the possibility of my catching her killer still existed.

For a few months after her death, while the police were still actively pursuing the case, I held out hope that I could still get revenge on her murderer. I reasoned that even if they apprehended him before I was able to locate him myself, I would still have the opportunity to eventually confront him face-to-face, either in jail, in court, or even in prison. During that time, the likelihood of getting revenge was still a possibility for me. As the months wore on, however, this option appeared more and more remote.

In any police investigation, the best chance of identifying and apprehending the offender occurs within the first few days. Beyond that point, the odds of success decrease significantly—the longer the time frame, the less likely the capture.

I knew that in Mother's case, the sheriff's office had run out of leads by the end of the first six months. From a purely pragmatic standpoint, they had worked all available clues without success, at which point her case had gone to the "too hard" file.

Like all investigative agencies, they reminded me in our later conversations that murder investigations are never closed. However, as an ex-officer, I knew that once our case was shelved, the person we sought would be captured only through some fluke of circumstance. This would be most likely in conjunction with the commission of another offense. Since I believed he was a serial murderer, driven by sexual-psychological impulses, I had no doubt that he would act again. The overriding question was *where* and *when* he would strike.

Once I was confident the police investigation had played itself out, I initiated my contingency plan. I had spent months planning all my options in great detail, and I had no intention of giving up based solely upon what the police had or had not determined. I then retained a well-known private investigator in the Wichita area (who was ex-law enforcement), hoping that he would fare better than they had.

Hiring private investigative personnel has its advantages as well as limitations. They can put a largely full-time effort into any one case, can expedite some activities, and often have influential contacts who can assist with an investigation.

On the other hand, their services can become expensive over time. They do not usually have access to critical police forensic data, and are legally required to turn over to the police any information that might lead to an arrest. Despite these limitations, I had promised myself from the outset that I would exclude no possible action in this investigation.

My investigator was very conscientious and explored as many avenues of research as he could, such as videotaping Mother's estate sale, placing ads for her missing personal items in the newspaper, and chasing down miscellaneous leads.

It was his contention that the key to the entire case was the porcelain Mardi Gras–type mask that the killer had placed on Mother's face during some psychotic ritual after her death. My investigator was convinced that this mask held some psychological clue to the killer's motives. Unfortunately, during the months of his effort, this was never substantiated. All other possibilities he explored also yielded no success.

Before I gave up, however. I had additional contingencies planned that I set in motion. Near the Thanksgiving holidays, I contacted the Wichita news media and arranged another trip back for purposes of talking to the local newspaper and television stations. Both offered detailed coverage, including announcement of the $10,000 reward, which we continued to offer for any useful information in the case. Other than an initial flurry of activity around largely useless leads, this effort also produced nothing.

It was obvious that this psychotic had told no one, since nobody stepped forward with useful information in return for a significant amount of money. This confirmed my theory that he was intelligent enough to avoid the common temptation of bragging to someone about his accomplishment.

This meant that my next option would be to conduct surveillance of Mother's residence on the anniversary date of her murder. But that would not be possible until after the first of the year. In the interim, all I could do was feed on my obsession for revenge to provide myself the energy I needed to survive an existence that was becoming more futile daily.

I believe that most victims share my demand that someone ensure just punishment for those responsible for their loss. Therefore, many survivors experience a nearly insatiable desire for revenge, which they may cling to for years.

They are unconcerned with the socioeconomic factors that lead criminals to choose violence as a lifestyle. They are sick of hearing about how tough life was for these reprobates in their youth. They are unmoved by any mitigating circumstances that supposedly led to the commission of their crimes. Their sole concern is that whoever condemned them to life sentences of emotional hell be forced to answer either to themselves, the courts, or God.

To many homicide survivors, the only acceptable form of justice is to witness the death of the one responsible for their loss (preferably slowly and painfully by their own hands). While forgiveness is a central tenet of Christianity, many survivors I know, including practicing Christians, would be satisfied with nothing less than personal revenge. Obviously, such unrealistic expectations place the victim or survivor in a no-win situation, because no matter what the ultimate outcome, no punishment will be enough to satisfy their thirst for personal vengeance.

Unfortunately for most crime victims today, their hope for achieving retribution through the legal system also remains largely unfulfilled. They rightfully demand that their offenders be made to pay for what they have done, and the court system represents their only legitimate recourse. Sadly, not only does the justice system provide them little satisfaction in this respect, but it does an equally poor job of even serving as a deterrent to lawless behavior.

The victim of spouse abuse recognizes that if her assailant is sentenced to fifteen years in prison, he will likely serve less than five. The victim of a violent robbery soon comes to understand that his case will, as often as not, be plea-bargained down to a lesser charge. This makes it more likely that his attacker will be back in society within a short while. The survivor of a murdered family member knows that even if the murderer is apprehended, the perpetrator can be sentenced to capital punishment in only some states. The family of a slain police officer realizes that even if his killer is given a "life" sentence, it will often be served in less than seven years, often less in states like Florida and Texas with their perceived revolving-door prison systems.

Additionally, as a result of the exhausting and lengthy appeals process in all capital cases, any legal trifle can be used as a justification for overturning a conviction. In my estimation, one of the most outrageous abuses of this appeals process occurred through the actions of the Florida Supreme Court in the 1988 case of *Robert Cox*.

Cox was originally convicted of killing nineteen-year-old Sharon Zellers. She had been on her way home from work at Walt Disney World one night when she somehow came in contact with him. He allegedly killed her and stuffed her body down a utility man-hole.

Evidence presented by the prosecution seemingly left little doubt that Cox had in fact committed the murder. Most damaging to the defense was forensic evidence presented by the prosecution that clearly demonstrated that the victim had bitten off the tip of Cox's tongue during their struggle. The jury obviously saw little doubt of his guilt, and he was convicted in less than ten hours' deliberation, and subsequently sentenced to the electric chair.[1]

The ultimate outcome of this case is particularly scandalous to me, however—and not because it involved the use of the typical legal appeals trivia. My anger stems from the fact that Florida's Supreme Court ultimately ruled the whole trial invalid. Incredibly, according to its opinion, there had not been enough evidence to justify the original conviction! In my estimation, these justices had in effect said that the members of the jury were incapable of determining for themselves whether the defendant was innocent or guilty. This court illustrated here that the rights of a convicted murderer are more important than making him pay for his crime and preventing him from repeating it. (Cox was eventually convicted of armed robbery and has since been sentenced to prison in the State of Texas.)

For anyone not scarred by violence, the rage experienced by victims in light of these endless travesties is incomprehensible. Those of us who are survivors, however, will agonize over these injustices for the remainder of our lives.

As victims, we realize we have been condemned to a future devoid of those who meant everything to us. Without recourse, our lives have been irrevocably altered by the selfish, vile side of humankind, which has inflicted pain and suffering on this earth for thousands of years. Such a fate is true futility in every sense of the word.

Victims of violence, unlike our offenders, get no second chances. We get no benefit of the doubt, we can seek no legal technicalities that may mitigate our fate. We have no hope of parole, probation, or pardon. Instead, we have been sentenced, arbitrarily and mercilessly to a lifetime of grief, torment, and regret by those who never once gave the slightest consideration to our wants, needs, or hopes.

Sooner or later, all survivors must confront the terrible reality that there is ultimately no way our victimization can ever be rightfully avenged. No court verdict, no financial compensation, no remorse on the part of our offenders—not even the death by our own hands of those responsible for our loss—can ever replace what has been taken from us.

I realize that the only thing that would satisfy me would be to get my mother back and resume the once-normal lifestyle I forfeited the day she died. Yet I know this can never happen—she is gone from my life in this world forever, and nothing can ever alter this dreadful reality for me.

This is why any victim's demand for vengeance ultimately proves to be a false and elusive goal. We must eventually face the painful fact that what has been done to us can never be undone, and life, as we once knew it, is over.

***

During those arduous months of futile investigative work, I began struggling with another question that further undermined my Christian faith. If God loved this world enough to give up His own Son for the sake of our lives (John 3:16), how could He have allowed the value of life to become as cheap as it is today?

The evidence to support this tragic fact seemed everywhere around me. A drunk driver gets in his car with a .25 percent blood alcohol level and kills two dozen teenagers when he smashes into their church bus. A group of bystanders cheers on a murderer as she repeatedly stabs the life out of her victim. Several black youths execute two white teenagers because they were out with a black female. Two white men set fire to a black man because of his race. A crazed murderer rapes and butchers five college students, placing the head of one victim on a bookshelf for shock value.[2] Terrorists blow a 747 out of the sky, killing 270 people to make a political statement. A woman happens upon a drug deal and is shot because she represents a potential witness. A disgruntled postal worker arms himself to the teeth and methodically executes fourteen people. Two aimless drifters accost a brother and a sister out camping, rape her repeatedly and slit his throat before beating him to death.[3] A group of youths push their friend into the path of an oncoming train for fun. Muggers beat an old woman to death for the $5 she has in her purse. A serial killer rapes and murders a dozen young boys, then cuts up their bodies to feed to his dogs.[4]

As cases such as this illustrate, we are now at a point where there are very few places left to hide from crime anymore. We hear increasingly about people being killed in their homes, in traffic, in the workplace, in restaurants, and even in church. As a matter of statistical fact, it is considerably more difficult to successfully rob a bank today than it is to get away with murdering another person.

In our watered-down legal system, the punishment for robbing a bank is also more likely to be more severe than the legal consequence of taking a life. Further, according to one former FBI agent, the national clearance rate (cases in which arrests are made) for murder thirty years ago was nearly 90 percent. Today that figure is barely over 60 percent, meaning nearly every other murder goes unsolved.

Other statistics substantiate the fact that we are indeed losing the battle being waged against violence in this country today. The amount of violent crime (defined as rape, robbery, violent assault, and murder) has increased 531 percent since 1960.[5] Interpreted from a personal level, this means that five out of every six twelve-year-old boys today will become the victims of violent crime sometime within their lifetimes. It means that any male born after 1974 now stands a greater chance of becoming a homicide victim than a U.S. soldier had of dying in World War II.[6]

The preponderance of violence surrounding us has also instilled a sense of fear and callousness in many people. This perception is common to most homicide survivors with whom I have spoken. They share my contention that people have become so accustomed to hearing and reading about violence and death that their fear and apathy sometimes cause them to ignore even hideous events occurring around them.

I recall a lady in one meeting describing how her brother had been stabbed repeatedly by one of his friends in a cocaine-induced frenzy. Although the victim screamed repeatedly within hearing distance of a number of residences, no one bothered to call the police until well after the assailant had fled the area. She kept asking the group almost rhetorically, "How could anyone hear his screaming and not do something? How could anybody be so uncaring?"

My faith during that period of time was slowly being eroded by my belief that this violent madness threatened to devour us all. Evil was allowed to triumph over good; wrong continued to trample over right; the innocents were being consumed by the guilty; and God even allowed the devil to spit in His face and laugh about it.

And I could only shake my head and wonder, *How long, Lord? How long must it take before the innocent are avenged?*

CHAPTER 6

SUFFOCATING IN A VACUUM OF LONELINESS AND ISOLATION

Know then that God has put me in the wrong,
and closed his net about me.
Behold, I cry out, "Violence!" but I am not answered;
I call aloud, but there is no justice…
He breaks me down on every side, and I am gone,
and my hope has He pulled up like a tree.

—Job 19:6–10

As 1991 inched to a close, I felt that I had been cast adrift on a sea of emotional emptiness, isolation, and loneliness. My frustration and anger increased with every dead end in the investigation, my hopes for revenge diminished by the day as a result, and my bitterness and resentment distorted my perspective of the world and everyone in it.

Of course, my day-to-day activities provided the illusion of normalcy. After all, fighting to contain the jungle of growth that Florida yards represented to my lawn business was a career in itself. I was also traveling long distances with my management consulting work, as well as handling Mother's estate while I was home. Added to all this were the countless hours I continued to pour into her case. Between working the investigation and managing the estate, I eventually made six trips back to Kansas that year alone.

Still, I recognized that my relationship with the world around me had already changed forever. I evaluated everything in terms of one horrible act that controlled my existence, and the focus of everything I thought, did, or said was in relation to my loss.

I avoided attending social functions, I often had no desire to go to church, my contacts with friends were very limited, and concentrating on the delivery of my professional training programs took every ounce of my will power.

I realized that even when I was in the presence of my family, I was in reality living alone emotionally. Since the first month after Mother's death, Nan and I spoke less and less about the case or its impact on our lives. I appeared to doubt she could fully accept what it had done to me, and she didn't think I wanted her support. I talked with Amy and Jason occasionally, but after a while, I felt there was little left for anyone to say.

Night after night, I sat alone in the garage after dark, listening as country music's best melancholy reinforced my conviction that sooner or later, we do all wind up alone.

One of the most painful insights of that time, though, was my feeling that I had been abandoned by those around me when I most needed them. It seemed that everyone—people at church, my customers, my wife's coworkers, even my business partner—avoided mentioning Mother's murder, as if it were a contagious disease and they would be the next to contract it.

Brief encounters with friends, and even extensive travel with my former business partner were characterized by a deafening silence on the subject. The unspoken questions that I felt hung in peoples' minds were seldom verbalized, evidenced only through episodes of awkward small talk.

Unfortunately, this quickly escalated into a cycle characterized by my increased withdrawal from others, which only compounded their uneasiness and avoidance of my true feelings.

Any meaningful self-disclosure on my part at that time was therefore limited to a select few individuals. My friend Duane had offered his assistance by driving up from Dallas to meet me in Wichita while I tried to piece the facts together shortly after the murder. My sister and I talked often throughout that year in our efforts to close the estate. I also made vain attempts to communicate with Nan, who was always willing to listen; but the rage controlling my life inhibited most of my best efforts to communicate with her.

As a result, the person with whom I found I could always express the depths of my depression and despair was my friend Carl. He and I had been friends twenty-five years, dating back to the days when we knocked each other down on the football field in Wichita as we competed for the same position. That bond of understanding has remained intact across all the miles and years, and I felt that only he could truly understand another male's emotions accompanying a loss like mine.

He alone would call me without fail every week, for months, and listen patiently as I described my slow descent into a world of hopelessness and disillusionment. His belief that I was headed down a one-way street to emotional oblivion prompted repeated urgings from him that I seek some type of mental health counseling. Sadly, Nan had suggested this for months; but it wasn't until Carl forced me to agree to see someone that I finally followed through with it.

I am convinced that such feelings of loneliness and isolation are shared almost universally by victims. I have heard countless survivors express frustration in not being given the opportunity to share their true emotions with other people. Their experiences support my contention that most people either choose to ignore the subject of our loss altogether, or approach it superficially at best. Nearly all participants in survivor meetings shared my observation that they felt they made others very uncomfortable, to the point that they were sometimes shunned and avoided completely. Many have stated that they were surprised to find out who their true friends really were. More often than not, these revelations led to termination of previously close relationships.

The book of Job, again, provides some insight into our struggle with adversity and how it affects our relations with others. It describes Job's lengthy discussion with his three friends who joined him to offer

THE SHADOW OF EVIL

support. Their intentions appeared initially to be good, as it is described they wept with him, tore their robes, and sat with him wordlessly for seven days (Job 2:11-13). In terms of empathetic support, one cannot do much better than this story describes. However, once Job initiated conversation, their conclusions regarding the source of his misery quickly began to alter the tone of their discussion.

Each of Job's friends attempted to offer his own insights into the reasons for his distress; but ultimately, none was able to come to an acceptable conclusion as to why this calamity had befallen their friend.

They often skirted the issue directly, instead choosing to remind Job of the greatness of God and the perfectness of His actions. They seemed content to remind him that his faith would get him through, and that he should try to accept all this as God's will. They seemed to discount the depths of his despair as they made shallow references to better days ahead and the need for his reliance on God's wisdom. Their frustrations increased once they realized they still could find no justification for Job's circumstances from any perspective.

Their demeanor eventually turned to anger and self-righteousness as they implied that Job must have done or said something to bring God's wrath down upon him. Surely, they insisted, He would not punish an innocent man. They ultimately denounced Job for questioning God's ways, and told him that he would surely be judged harshly for daring to do so himself.

The implications of this intense theological debate should offer good advice for those who attempt to aid survivors. Whether as mental health professionals, or as friends and family of victims, we must offer unconditional, nonjudgmental support for those in this distress.

I believe any attempt to reach firm conclusions why such tragic circumstances occur is self-defeating for all involved. The fact is that the *why*'s surrounding any act of violence simply stem from man's inherent evil and his desire to dominate others. Beyond that, I don't believe there are any real answers. Therefore, our approach should be to provide any possible emotional assistance we can—simply being available and willing to listen when asked.

Because most friends and family members lack the skills to provide sufficient emotional support for survivors, they must recognize the importance of taking the initiative in directing their loved one toward appropriate available resources. As soon after the funeral as possible, they should begin determining which community support services are available. Their efforts to influence their loved one to seek assistance at the appropriate time should be gentle, but persistent.

I believe it is imperative that those surviving any act of violence be encouraged to connect with external support systems as soon as possible. I do not agree, however, with those who feel that a homicide survivor can be satisfactorily assimilated into a therapy group as soon as one week after their loss. I maintain that there should be some "safe period" (i.e., three to six weeks) in which the bereaved have some modicum of time to adjust in their own ways to their circumstances. Otherwise, I think their emotional stability can be subject to question; and the benefits they derive from the group experience, as well as their contributions to the others in this setting, could be compromised.

Many survivors, particularly males, are adamant that they "don't need anybody's help," that "no one else could possibly understand," and that "it wouldn't do any good anyway." It is my contention that such attitudes are in large part the result of social programming that teaches that "real men" don't eat quiche, ask for directions, cry in public, or get emotional assistance from anybody. Perhaps this offers some insight into why fewer men are active in homicide support groups than are women, and I suspect this may lead to a higher incidence of long-term male emotional maladjustment.

Beyond gender issues, however, lies a bigger factor that I believe is responsible for resistance by many to such group support processes. Our society still maintains some vestiges of the old belief that people who seek mental health assistance are "ill" or "disturbed." Therefore, some members of both sexes refuse help for fear of having such a stigma placed upon them.

For instance, I was discriminated against by a major insurance company, which denied me disability coverage on the basis that I take antidepressant medication. Such myopic attitudes and medieval practices, coupled with victims' ongoing sense of isolation from others, represent a potentially deadly obstacle in the path to restoring survivors' long-term mental health.

The overwhelming sense of futility accompanying the suffering caused by violence is all but impossible for non-survivors to appreciate. Survivors' former routine lives have been overwhelmed with a sense of hopelessness. This despair pervades their entire existence because their suffering is so unnecessary. While death through car accidents, illness, and war are tragic, and surviving family members will always search for reasons why, nowhere is the sense of dying in vain more evident than when someone is killed by the actions of another. All sense of purpose to life and any hope of order to the universe is shaken when we are forced to accept such unmitigated futility.

From my own experience, I believe that this fatalistic perspective of life greatly influences a survivor's tendency to become cynical toward the world in general, and often jealous and resentful of others around him. Why should survivors not react with bitterness and resentment toward a world that has robbed them of someone they loved?

They know that relatively few people are forced to deal with their unique type of grief, and that only those who have can truly understand the magnitude of their loss. They see people all around them enjoying loving relationships now denied them by a criminal element of society that operates largely unchecked by societal or legal restraints. They are appalled when they read about monsters who molest and murder children; animals who rape, rob, and kill; societal misfits who kidnap innocent people or go on murderous rampages for reasons known only to them.

Sometimes this cynicism results in survivors demonstrating considerable insecurity, anxiety, and even paranoia, about living in such a violent society. Any prior illusion of security or personal well-being has been destroyed by the reality that violence has devastated their world once, and nothing prevents it from happening again.

Parents who have lost a child may become overprotective of the siblings, often to the point of obsession. A spouse may interpret any tardiness of her mate in terms of the most dire consequences. Children sometimes display great fear of being alone and may demonstrate other regressive behaviors.

Although I perhaps represent the exception, I personally experienced little, if any, fear for myself after my mother's murder. Because I knew her killer had kept her purse as a souvenir for purposes of subsequent sexual titillation, I recognized that he could easily locate me if he desired. As a result, I actually relished the unlikely possibility that he would decide to come after me, thus allowing me the opportunity to kill him under legally and morally justifiable terms.

My sister, on the other hand, had repeated violent nightmares about this, and was desperately fearful that this person would decide to stalk her at some point in the future.

My fears for my family, however, were intense. This was not so much out of anxiety about Mother's killer coming back but from fear of the countless sociopaths walking the streets of Orlando or any other city today. When my wife was late coming home from anywhere, my mind immediately conjured up images of terrifying possibilities, and I was always on edge until she returned.

Much worse was my apprehension for my son and my daughter. I insisted on knowing where they were from one moment to the next. I always felt a sense of anxiety when my son rode off to school on his bicycle in the morning, or when my daughter went out at night with her friends. If they were so much as one minute late getting home at an appointed time, they knew that they would face an irate father upon their return.

This obsession with their safety once led to an incident that, in retrospect, is somewhat humorous but which could have been tragic at the time. Nan had convinced me to attend dinner with several friends from church one Saturday evening, and I hesitantly agreed. Before we had even finished dinner, I called home to check on the kids. After calling repeatedly and getting busy signals, I knew that something must be wrong, because we have call waiting service that eliminates these tones. I quickly left the dinner and roared home at warp speeds, only to find our residence alarm wailing, and both Amy and Jason gone.

I was trying to fight back panic with the alarm screaming in my ears when I noticed that our bedroom door was closed, knowing it had been open when we left. Almost beside myself at that point, I was hesitant to go into our room. Instead, I raced into the garage and grabbed the first thing I could find, which was a yard rake, and decided it would have to do. Upon checking our bedroom and finding the telephone off the hook, I heard a loud knock on the front door. Without thinking about who it might be, I threw the door open and lunged out with the rake, only to discover a patrolman from the Orlando Police Department standing there with a startled look on his face. I must have scared him as much as he did me, because his hand made a movement toward his gun, at which point I quickly identified myself and apologized.

As it turned out, Amy had been in our bedroom using the phone just after we left. Our dog had apparently knocked the receiver off the hook shortly after that. Through some bizarre coincidence, something else had set off our alarm once the kids had left for the evening, thus initiating the whole fiasco. We sorted everything out after the fact, but I was forced to recognize that my obsession with their safety in that instance could have been catastrophic for me.

***

Regardless of the exact nature of our emotional sojourn subsequent to our encounter with violence, many of us ultimately arrive at a destination of extreme depression and total desperation. It is not uncommon for survivors to become so overwhelmed with their circumstances that at times they question the purpose of continuing to live. They recognize that recovery from their devastating loss represents a lifetime effort, and they may come to doubt that such an arduous emotional recovery process is worth the struggle.

These emotions represent another paradox to those professing Christianity. On one hand, we have lived our entire lives believing that God would supply all our needs, and that He would sustain us through any ordeal. Yet our existence at this point consists entirely of immense emotional pain, an intolerable sense of loss, and unshakable doubts surrounding the Christian values we have embraced for a lifetime.

Where, then, is our faith in action? What value is it to us when every day represents unending emotional torture? Where is the God we have always worshiped and trusted, when we need Him most? Why won't He do something to alleviate our unbearable pain and sorrow?

At that point in time, with the darkest hours of my life bearing down on me like a freight train in the night, I knocked desperately on God's door... and heard only the sound of it being locked and double-locked from within.

CHAPTER 7

BETRAYED BY THE WORLD AND GOD HIMSELF

Why didst thou bring me forth from the womb?
Would that I had died before any eye had seen me...
Let me alone, that I may find a little comfort
before I go whence I shall not return...

—Job 10:18–21

I had not quite given up on this world and God's role in it as the first anniversary of Mother's murder approached. I had managed somehow to suffer through the ordeal of our first Christmas without her, although that holiday season was almost intolerable. Probably the only thing that made it bearable was the fact that I spent Christmas Eve putting together our family history from all the photos and archives we had retrieved from her home earlier that summer.

All my thoughts after the holidays were then focused on the anniversary of her murder and the possibility of confronting her killer, which that occasion represented. Even though I knew it would be a small-odds chance, there still remained a slim possibility that whoever killed her would make an appearance somewhere in the area that weekend. Perhaps it would be at her house, near the bridge where he had dumped her body, or even at the cemetery.

Since my trip back to Kansas for this purpose had been months in the planning, I was well prepared before I set out. I packed cold-weather clothes for the expected inclement Kansas weather in January. I included binoculars for observation of the area, as well as flashlights for staying out all night. My investigator even supplied me with a mobile radio to stay in contact with Mother's friend, Tom, who would be working with me in every phase of this effort.

The most ominous prospect of the trip, though, was evident as I loaded my shotgun into the car. I wasn't making this trip with the intent of obtaining my own vigilante justice, in spite of the fact that nothing would have given me more pleasure. My intention, should I discover the perpetrator, was simply to apprehend him, ensure that he divulged to me his motives and actions that night, and then turn him over to the sheriff's office.

Still, the ex-cop part of me knew that confronting an experienced killer would be a high-risk activity, and that he would not willingly submit to being captured, much less freely disclose what he knew. I was, therefore, prepared to do anything necessary, both to protect myself and to ensure that he went to jail, so I was taking no chances. My midnight-black 12-gauge combat shotgun represented my best insurance policy in that respect. I intended to keep it within arm's reach throughout that weekend, and I was emotionally prepared to use it if necessary.

Actually, the decision of whether or not I could ever use deadly force against another person had been made much earlier while I was in police work. I had decided all those years ago that if it ever came down to taking another life to protect my own or someone else's, I would do it without hesitation. Fortunately, my resolve in this respect had never been tested to that point, although it had come close on a number of occasions.

The situation I was facing in this circumstance, however, was radically different. I was now an ordinary citizen, no longer a law enforcement officer. While I had a permit to carry a weapon within the state of Florida, even having that gun in my car constitutes a third-degree felony in many states. Additionally, I would be actively stalking the murderer of my mother—not exactly an ideal legal posture for me should push comes to shove. Additionally, I knew this surveillance effort represented a very real element of danger to me, given the circumstances.

While I was willing to take whatever chances existed in all of this, I was still greatly concerned about my motives and their possible consequences. I knew that as a Christian I would ultimately be accountable to God for anything that might result from such an encounter. Therefore, it was critical that I discern exactly what my purposes and intentions were in this situation before I left.

After a lot of prayer and soul-searching, I was satisfied with my conscience that I was prepared to kill only under terms that would be legally and morally justifiable. Still, any number of unexpected contingencies could conceivably occur, and I recognized that some chance existed that he or I could die as a result.

Saying good-bye to my family as I set out across the country under these circumstances was therefore difficult. Nevertheless, I had determined from the outset that I would do anything necessary to ensure that Mother's murderer was brought to account, so I refused to compromise.

Tom and I had constructed a very detailed plan of surveillance, which we executed with precise accuracy. We were aided by one of our investigator's staff, so among the three of us, we were able to keep the house, bridge, and cemetery in constant visual contact. We all had mobile radios so that we could communicate with each other, either routinely or in case of an emergency.

Since Friday, January 17, was the anniversary by day, and Saturday, the eighteenth, was the anniversary by date, we stayed out until very late both nights. We would move between positions, but rarely was any one location out of someone's sight.

My emotions throughout the weekend alternated between anxious excitement and tedious boredom. After the first few hours of hopeful anticipation wore off, I settled into an emotional routine that was monotonous and surprisingly devoid of fear. Nevertheless, I had it timed that I could get the shotgun out from under the back seat within three seconds if necessary.

I spent most of the first evening watching the bridge. As I sat there during those late hours of the night, I mentally replayed the monstrous set of circumstances that had occurred exactly one year earlier that night.

As near as we could determine, Mother's assailant had entered her home late that evening by some unknown means. We had never been able to establish with any certainty where his point of entry had been. He had, however, made it appear as if he had come in the rear glass door, by throwing a huge concrete block through the glass. However he accomplished his entry, I suspected he came in with that frightful Mardi Gras mask on for purposes of terrorizing and overcoming her through this element of surprise.

I shuddered to think of what happened after that, although I knew that most serial killers relish their murderous acts by prolonging them. Therefore, I could hardly force myself to accept the likelihood that her death may not have been quick.

I surmised that after her death, he spent some time engaging in bizarre ritualistic behaviors that had meaning only for him. These included piling her shoes in a corner, setting her orthopedic pillows upon one another, gathering small personal items that represented trophies of his accomplishment and binding her body with knotted pantyhose.

I also suspected that he had gone to great lengths to stage the crime scene both to mislead the police and demonstrate his contempt for them. I knew this would have represented a high-risk activity for him, because he would have been spending additional time in her residence, thus increasing the odds of his being discovered. He had ultimately removed her body from the house and used her vehicle to drive her body to the site at which I now sat.

It was readily evident to me why Mother's killer had picked that particular spot to dump her body. It was ten miles north of town, and another six or seven miles west. A solitary farmhouse was located a quarter of a mile to my east and another sat about a half mile away, over a small rise to the west.

He had run virtually no risk that night in appearing at this particular sight to abandon her body because of the remote nature of this location. No one in either residence could have seen or heard him, especially if he had entered the area with his lights off, as he most likely did. The chances of anyone happening by that secluded section of gravel road after midnight were practically nil, so the two or three minutes it would have taken him to finish the devil's work represented practically no danger to him.

Like most experienced killers, he had been shrewd and calculating. I had no doubt that he had chosen this place as his dump site well in advance, probably several weeks prior to her murder. Deciding upon this location had probably occurred soon after he resolved in his sick mind to make her his next target. He had left few loose ends in his preparation, and that had paid off for him in the long run.

The moonlight created what seemed to me to be an almost surrealistic landscape that night. A large row of barren hedge trees stood on the other side of the road, casting ghostly shadows over fields of wheat stubble. Winter had robbed every tree of its foliage, creating a countryside that looked bleak and desolate, and to me, desperately lonely. The rocks lining the creek bed where she had lain gave off an eerie glow of pale reflected moonlight.

What struck me as most strange, though, was the utter silence of the night. Living in the city for so long, I had almost forgotten how soundless nights are that far out in the country. Occasionally I heard the sound of a dog barking in the distance. At one point, I faintly heard the whisper of a jet flying high overhead toward some unknown destination, which I thought odd for such a late hour. For the most part, though, the wailing of the wind through the trees and the howling of a pack of coyotes was my only accompaniment on that lonesome evening.

Only at one point did fear become a significant factor to me. After I had sat there long enough for the still silence to begin to unnerve me, I began to question whether I had the courage to get out of the car and walk down into that creek bed. That spot of ground that had so callously held her body for two weeks represented a huge emotional obstacle to me.

JEFFREY M. DAVIS

Could I step out of my car and back into time to that night one year ago exactly, and walk over to the same spot where he had disposed of her lifeless body? Would I be able to handle it emotionally as I stood at the very location where he completed his demon's mission by dumping my mother's precious body out on the ground like some bag of garbage for the animals to root through?

At that moment, I realized that my apprehension was not of the fiend responsible for my mother's death. Whatever fear I felt came not from him, but from knowing that I might be incapable of confronting this particular reality of her loss. I was no longer 1,500 miles away, dealing with this abstract horror over the telephone. I was walking the same ground her murderer had walked. I was hearing the same sounds he had heard. I was now experiencing firsthand, in every detail, my own portion of that same terror that accompanied my mother's death. I wasn't sure I was man enough under those frightening circumstances to breathe the same air exhaled exactly one year earlier by this nameless, faceless monster of my own mind's creation.

Before I could talk myself out of it, I grabbed the door handle and jumped out, heading across the road and down into the dry creek bed.

I searched the area for some time, still looking for long-gone signs of his presence. I walked under the bridge that had been so effective at shielding Mother's body from view until one boy's dog had pursued something under there.

My senses—smell, hearing, sight, even touch—were working at capacity, forcing me to soak in the dreadful reality of the moment.

I thought of how ironic it would have been had this phantom I had been pursuing for so long appeared at that moment. There I would have been, unarmed and alone, one hundred yards away from my radio and my shotgun. What a confrontation that would have been. A demon from hell back to enjoy his handiwork, and the son of one of his victims bent on ensuring the downfall of his mother's murderer, alone together, eye-to-eye, face-to-face. Two animals pitted against each another, no way out and no road back—one wins and one loses. One of life's oldest dramas, the battle for survival in its most primal form, would have been played out right there, with the only spectators being the devil and God Himself.

I pondered hard on how it might have ended, but only the wind in the trees offered a response.

That mental confrontation was as close to Mother's murderer as I would get that weekend. From that point on, everything we did turned out to be largely anticlimactic. My hopes for success in that endeavor waned with each passing hour—no contact at the cemetery, none at the bridge, and nothing at the house.

Unlike the surroundings near the bridge, the amount of activity near her house shocked me. As we swapped surveillance details and Tom assumed responsibility for watching the bridge and I the house, I could hardly believe the amount of traffic that passed during the course of the remainder of the evening. Mother's house was located on the northeast corner of a well-traveled east-west artery, north of town about six miles. During one five-minute period, I counted over thirty cars that went by. I assumed that this was a representative sample of what would have occurred the night of her murder and wondered how her killer could have accomplished his mission so easily.

The ease with which we were able to watch the movements of the people who had since occupied her house was what surprised me most. We were able to park our cars out behind her house in the parking lot of a marine engine repair service, about fifty yards to the southeast. A large row of cedar trees obscured the south side of her house, and a single cedar stood just off of the patio, blocking part of that vantage point.

Still, with binoculars, we had visual access to a large part of the backyard; and in spite of the trees, we could see the lights in any room throughout the back part of the residence. From the street, we could watch any area in the front portion of the house.

During both of those nights, we knew when the occupants left, came home, put out the dog, and went to bed. Unfortunately, the activities of the occupants were all we saw, because the person we had hoped to observe never appeared.

Our surveillance activities confirmed what I had believed to be true all along—for a person with enough determination, it is incredibly easy to successfully stalk and murder someone else. All it takes is the right amount of motivation, patience, and planning.

Partial consensus of opinion among investigating personnel had always leaned toward the theory that Mother's killer had targeted her well in advance of actually carrying out his plan. Watching her residence those two nights substantiated my contention that he had been observing her for several weeks prior, noting her habit patterns in great detail to ensure success when the time came. It was both frightening and infuriating to realize that he had undoubtedly observed our every action during that last Christmas visit.

Any remaining hopes for success in apprehending the ghost of my life's nightmare waned with those last hours of Saturday night. What had once been cautious anticipation on my part was slowly turning into the ragged edge of frustration and failure, which I was certain would grate on me for a long time to come. I was forced to accept that my chances for achieving any closure in this ordeal were about as slim as my being able to return to Florida and forget that any of this ever happened.

As I lost sight of Mother's residence in my rear-view mirror that night, I fought off the desperation that came with recognizing I had few cards left to play in this, the highest-stakes game of my life. The thought of never seeing any end to this perpetual horror was unbearable, but that eventuality loomed increasingly larger with every mile on the long drive back home.

Although my spirits throughout that return trip were at a lifetime rock bottom, I had not yet sunk into my soon-to-be state of complete despair and desperation. This was because I believed I still held some semblance of control over this situation. I still felt that the war I was waging against Mother's murderer was not yet over. Although the future was looking increasingly bleak, I would not allow myself to give up because my list of contingencies had not yet been exhausted.

My best hopes for success still lay in convincing the *Unsolved Mysteries* television series personnel to broadcast the case, through which we might receive some critical piece of information from a viewer as a result. I had already submitted a detailed chronology of the case to them a few months earlier, so I kept trying to convince myself that I would receive some response fairly soon.

The lifestyle I resumed upon returning from my failed investigative effort became little more than an exercise in tedious survival. My motivation for doing anything was almost nonexistent. I pursued my business interests as before; I fulfilled my personal obligations as usual; I went through the motions of being a father and a husband. Still, any sense of vigor or enjoyment in life seemed to have died with my mother.

The perpetual sunshine of the warm Florida winter days was an insult to me. I wanted to live under the cold, gray overcast skies of Kansas winters that more appropriately characterized my futile existence. How dare the sun continue to shine and the birds sing, just as if nothing had happened? How could the world callously go on, as though she had never existed? It was my mother gone forever, and while her murder hadn't stopped the earth's revolution, it had knocked my world completely off its axis, and I knew that it could never be righted again.

It became more and more of an effort just to plod through another day. I realized that I wasn't really living, as most people would define it. I was just going through the motions of existing. More often than not, I didn't care whether I got out of bed in the morning. I could find little reason to invest my energies in anything. Depression, in the most profound sense of the word, had become my way of life.

My business interests served as a good diversion at times, especially when I was traveling. But invariably, I returned home to the same unanswered questions, the same intolerable sense of injustice, and the overwhelming pall of bitterness and resentment that draped my world.

I also knew that I was destroying not only myself, but also those relationships that mattered most to me. Yet my anger and depression fed upon each other continually, until the cumulative effects of these eventually dominated my existence.

No matter what I did, I could not extricate myself from the grip of this emotional morass. I prayed for relief, and sometimes saw some short-term improvement. Nevertheless, it was only a matter of time before the anger or depression won out and I was right back to seeing the world from the bottom of a sewage pit again.

I became enraged over the simplest things, lashed out at anyone around me (usually the family), and then sank into a state of intolerable despair because of my shameful lack of self-control. Most frustrating of all was recognizing that I had less control over my own life at this point than I originally had over the circumstances responsible for this nightmare.

Eventually, I learned that much of my problem was attributable to clinical depression, which previously I had been familiar with only through reading. Fortunately, I had begun seeing a Christian counselor some months prior to my last trip to Kansas. We had established an excellent rapport, and during the course of our counseling sessions, I felt comfortable discussing with him all that was affecting my life. At one point, he referred me to a psychiatrist for the purpose of determining if medication would provide me any relief.

Like many others in such circumstances, I experienced some trepidation at the thought of actually consulting a psychiatrist. Having my master's degree in counseling psychology, I knew better than most victims that these medical specialists were an appropriate resource for these situations, especially where biochemical factors may be involved. Still, seeing a counselor was one thing; but the thought of actually being evaluated by a head doctor was something else.

This being the reaction from one familiar with the mental health field, I can only guess the number of survivors who are denying themselves access to critically important resources because of these same apprehensions. Not only might the cost of these services represent one prohibitive factor, but the stigma attached to utilizing mental health expertise may also deter people from seeking help. Add to this the aversion some people have to taking prescription drugs for emotional conditions, and the bottom line is that many victims continue to suffer intense depression that could probably have been alleviated relatively easily.

My observation from attending survivors' meetings is that the majority of victims do not receive long-term mental health assistance. I sense that the only support many of these people receive is that provided by other survivors within this group setting. I am by no means implying that such support is ineffective. On the contrary, organizations such as Parents of Murdered Children, the National Victim Center, the National Organization for Victim's Assistance, and the Bereaved Survivors of Homicide group (Orlando local) offer a support system for victims that cannot be achieved through any other format.

These support groups offer the type of safe, open, and honest environment in which survivors can freely express their sorrow, anger, loneliness, and the gamut of other emotions unique to victims. The strength of such a support system lies in the fact that all those participating have been forced to walk that lonely road known only to victims, so true empathy can be found here and here alone.

Only a survivor can truly understand what another victim is going through, and any honest mental health professional will quickly admit that. Still, psychological counseling services have proven to be helpful to many people under extreme duress and should not be dismissed offhand by hesitant victims as an inappropriate resource.

For persons like myself, access to medication is sometimes the only hope for alleviating chronic depression, thus effectively making professional counseling mandatory. The psychiatrist's assessment of my family history revealed that because my mother most likely suffered from biochemical depression, this same physiological condition was largely responsible for my own severe depression. He also concluded that I had probably fought this depressive state all my life without recognizing it for what it was.

This is why chronic, clinical depression is so insidious. Most people's understanding of "depression" is that it is some self-induced, short-term state of mind that can be eliminated with enough effort. The result is that many people, especially self-determinant ones like myself, feel that they should be able to control this emotion, and blame themselves mercilessly when they can't. Continued failure in this effort often sets up a recurrent cycle of self-recrimination, diminished self-esteem, further depression, often ending in total despair and hopelessness.

Clinical depression is far more common than most people would imagine. It is somewhat of a "good news/bad news" phenomenon. On the negative side, 25 percent of the United States female population and 10 percent of its male population will experience clinical depression at some point during their lives. Depression is also considered to be the underlying cause of most suicides in this country. However, somewhere between 80 and 90 percent of all depressed individuals respond to medical treatment, so there is cause for hope.[1]

For those family and friends suspecting this condition in a loved one, the symptoms are relatively easy to identify. These include feeling bad for an extended period of time, guilt, diminished sexual drive, reduced self-esteem, isolation, fatigue, anxiety, reduced appetite, insomnia or excessive sleep, irritability, and suicidal references...[2] If a number of these symptoms are present for an extended period of time, those concerned should pursue available resources as quickly as possible for their loved one's well-being. While depression is treatable, the consequences when it is left unattended can be dire.

***

I probably didn't bottom out in my own state of hopeless depression and despair until I was finally forced to admit that all the effort I had expended attempting to resolve my mother's murder had ultimately been for nothing. Having to concede defeat in this war for closure in Mother's case represented the most crushing loss I will ever experience.

Every day for almost fourteen months since that terrible phone call from my sister, I had planned and organized, analyzed and researched, acted and reacted in every way possible to make some sense of why my mother had to die. Relatively early in the investigative process, I had resigned myself to the fact that justice would probably never be served on her killer. Nevertheless, I held out hope that I could at least find some answers as to exactly what had happened that night, determine some motivation behind her killer's actions, or perhaps satisfy myself with some explanation of why it had to be her in particular.

Right up until that time when I finally ran out of options in my investigation, I kept telling myself I would never give up. I refused to even consider the possibility that I might actually lose the most important fight of my life to some nameless, murderous mistake of humanity. Even as the eternal pessimist, I maintained hope that all the money I had spent, the countless hours I had worked on the case, and my prayers seeking resolution would eventually pay off. To the bitter end, I would not accept the possibility that God would allow all of my effort to be for nothing, that He would refuse to recognize my efforts without providing something in return. Ultimately, however, my worst fear was realized—I would, in fact, be forced to live the remainder of my life without a single answer to the tormenting questions that consumed me.

My last hopes for resolution finally died with a phone call from a representative of the *Unsolved Mysteries* television series, who informed me that the producers had decided not to air our story. No reason was offered—actually, just that sometimes a seemingly good story is not determined to be airworthy. He went on to explain that the producers can only take a small portion of cases submitted, and only they know their criteria for selection. He himself hadn't even been informed as to why we had been rejected. He was sorry and all, but that was the reality of the television business.

As I hung up, I thought about the irony of it all. Everything I had worked for had just collapsed in unqualified failure, based in all probability upon how one television producer felt when he had gotten up that morning. It was almost laughable really—months and months of research, travel, phone calls, letters, surveillance, planning, and calculating had all ended with a sigh. I was at the end of my list of options, which meant my war for answers was over.

At that time, even I didn't realize what a profound impact this concession of failure would have on me. I tried to accept this as just one more in the endless series of disappointments and frustrations associated with Mother's death. I told myself that the odds for success in this effort had been overwhelming from the beginning. I tried to justify the outcome by reminding myself that thousands of people are murdered each year, that many of these cases remain unsolved forever, so my circumstance was nothing out of the ordinary in this day and age.

None of this logic would work, however, because I saw a bigger, much more important issue at stake. I was now obsessed with God's role in all my travails throughout this entire ordeal, specifically what He might have done for me to prevent this devastating failure.

From the outset, I had never held Him accountable for what had happened to my mother that night. I knew full well that evil people are capable of unspeakable acts, and that the devil himself, personified in the form of an emotionally twisted psychopath, was the one responsible for my loss. Even though I knew that God could have intervened on her behalf, and sometimes does so for others in similar circumstances, I never once blamed Him for what had happened. His degree of responsibility in all that had transpired since that time, however, was quite another matter.

I simply could find no way to justify how He could have ignored my repeated requests for answers and turned His back on me in my time of greatest need. I had been raised to believe that because I was a committed believer in Christ, He would always be with me throughout life whenever I needed Him. I had always tried to take Him at His word—if we seek, we will find; that if we knock, the door will be opened; that if we ask, we will receive. As far as I was concerned, I had certainly done my part in seeking, knocking, and asking... over and over and over, to absolutely no avail.

Where had all my prayers, faith, and effort gotten me? I looked around to find myself standing on the exact same terrain of grief and heartache where I had been an eternity ago as this horror first became reality. I had vainly believed when I started out on this desperate search for resolution that God would be with me every step of the way. Now that the smoke had cleared and the dust had settled, however, I found that He had silently slipped away and left me alone to grope blindly through the maze of anger, loneliness, frustration, and bitterness that marked my day-to-day existence.

THE SHADOW OF EVIL

My battle to ensure justice and find answers was over; and in its wake, I realized that I been abandoned by the One I most trusted and desperately needed. Forsaken, I was left alone to sift through the emotional debris of my life's worst defeat.

At no other point during my forty years had I ever been so overwhelmed by feelings of abandonment and betrayal. My existence personified absolute futility and hopelessness—my entire life had become a pointless exercise in despair and fatalistic resignation. I had failed at the most important task I would ever undertake, and knew in my heart that I would be doomed to a future of bitterness and animosity as a result. I doubted that I could ever see the world around me again, except through the distorted prism of cynical resentment.

Worst of all, I had to accept the fact that the God I had always believed I could rely on had moved out of my life and left no forwarding address.

PART II

THE LONG ROAD TO RECOVERY

Retribution often means that we eventually do to
ourselves what we have done unto others.

—Eric Hoffer

There is no such thing as justice—in or out of court.

—Clarence Darrow

Justice is the ligament which holds civilized
beings and nations together.

—Daniel Webster

Whenever a separation is made between liberty and justice,
neither, in my opinion is safe.

—*Edmund Burke*

Justice is the firm and continuous desire to
render to everyone that which is his due.

—*Justinian*

Whoever fights monsters should see to it that
he does not become a monster himself.
And when you look into the abyss, the abyss also looks into you.

—*Friedrich Nietzsche*

CHAPTER 8

THE FALLACY OF PLACING OUR EXPECTATIONS ON GOD

For the foolishness of God is wiser than men,
and the weakness of God is stronger than men.

—1 Corinthians 1:25

Since Mother's death, I have spent countless hours examining how this tragedy has permanently altered my life. A number of insights have become apparent that reflect fundamental changes in my beliefs about myself, the world we live in, and God's role in both. In retrospect, I feel that my willingness to challenge a lifetime of sometimes faulty assumptions unknowingly represented my first step in a long journey back to emotional health.

Since most of us are barraged with societal messages that suggest we settle for nothing but the best from life, we can very easily be seduced into believing that both life and God somehow owe us something. We may fall into the subconscious trap of expecting events to always work in our best interests. As practicing Christians, this mentality can easily translate into an expectation of God, which somehow assumes He will unfailingly direct the course of earthly events to the fulfillment of our individual desires. My own experience as a survivor leads me to believe that a fine line separates realistic faith in the power of God from the naive expectancy of harmonious life circumstances.

I now believe that many of us in our prosperous society adopt this unrealistic sense of expectation regarding the circumstances that impact us. I feel that it is hard to resist the belief that a lifetime of health, wealth, and happiness is somehow our birthright in this affluent nation. Over the course of our lives, if we come to subconsciously hold this expectation, then experiencing anything less may cause bitter disillusionment at some point in time.[1]

In his works on rational-emotive counseling therapies (RET), Albert Ellis maintains that much of our discontent can be attributed to our irrational or illogical interpretation of events affecting us.[2] My interpretation of his rational-emotive precepts in the context of surviving violence leads me to believe that we must eventually accept several painful but logical realities if we are ever to attain emotional healing subsequent to our loss.

First, we must recognize that the violent nature of our world places every one of us at risk of becoming a victim. Statistics confirm that violence has become a way of life in this country. Five million people are victims of serious crime annually.[3] The reality of today is that there is an increasingly large element of society that practices violence as a way of life and will not hesitate to kill another person without reason. In a rational context, then, we victims of violence simply represent the statistical realities of a violent world.

Compounding the problem of our sometimes-myopic perspective of circumstance may also be our tendency to believe that we have the ultimate control over our human destiny. I believe this is one of the greatest and most dangerous delusions of life. Many of us are taught from childhood that with the right amount of determination and effort, we have total charge over our own futures. Those whose lives have been drastically altered by an act of violence know that self-determination is simply one variable among many that ultimately determine the outcomes of our lives.

Even now, I still place a strong value on blazing my own trail, exerting my powers of influence and persuasion, and influencing events around me whenever possible. However, Mother's death and my bitter defeat in obtaining answers and ensuring justice on her behalf have forced me to change my perception of how much I can actually control my own world.

As much as my self-sufficient nature resists, I now must conclude that the role I play in shaping my destiny is much more limited than I once believed. I admit my future is more realistically a combination of several factors, of which my own effort is only one. Of greater significance, it now appears to me, are the brutal and unexpected circumstances we sometimes encounter, and the mysterious role that God's will plays in these.

One of the most profound questions I have struggled with in this respect is, by what means is His will actually carried out in our lives? Trying to determine how He works His will in a cruel and violent world remains a tremendously difficult issue for me to understand.

I struggle continually to maintain an active faith in the Lord of this universe who allows people to suffer horribly in a wicked world. While it would be much easier to blindly hold to the childlike perspective that "He has the whole world in His hands," the terrible realities of violence show me that this issue of His control is more complex.

Certainly, in the broadest sense, God does still control this world. At least He does in terms of having established the laws of physics that determine the motion of the earth within the solar system and our physical interaction as humans with our earthly environment.

Because of this fact, though, can we go on to assume that as the omnipotent universal force, He accounts for every action that is played out millions of times during the course of each day? Can we, as Christians, expect Him to go to bat for us in every circumstance we encounter? If so, should we then blame Him for our misfortunes or give Him blanket credit for every good event that affects us? My experience as a survivor has forced me to conclude otherwise.

As a result of my own encounter with violence, I now perceive the Lord's role in my life as much more powerful in an internal sense, but greatly diminished from an external context. By that, I mean that I now believe that He can exert a tremendous amount of influence within the life (heart or soul) of Jeff Davis, but that His role within those circumstances affecting my existence in this world is significantly less than I had once believed it to be.

In assessing the course of events over my lifetime, I am convinced that at certain critical junctures, He has indeed played a direct role in the outcome of circumstances. Career opportunities, business endeavors, personal successes, and other events have transpired in such unusual ways that coincidence, luck, logic, and other explanations are insufficient, in and of themselves, to explain the results. The issue in question, then, is not did He influence my life but, rather, how He did so.

Did He directly dictate my own thoughts and actions, or those with whom I was interacting, to provide me that particular job, or cause that specific financial gain, or allow me that given opportunity? Perhaps in some instances this was, in fact, what occurred.

But I tend to believe that His influence was wielded primarily in these instances via a more subtle, "behind the scenes" manner in which He was indirectly influencing me through my conscience, thought processes, and powers of good judgment. To me, this seems more plausible than envisioning Him reordering the laws of nature, dictating human will, or physically redirecting a certain course of events specifically for my gain or benefit.

This is why I now believe that for the most part, whenever He chooses to exert His impact on our lives, His method for so doing is largely centered around "speaking" to our inner selves. That is, I see His role as a more subtle effort to influence our individual actions, not dictate a certain course of events that He deems to be in our best interests.

This thought may be distressing to many believing Christians who have always attributed every stroke of luck or good fortune in this world to our Father's beneficent hand favoring them. While in some cases this may be so, I believe that attributing such broad scope of circumstance directly to God can be dangerous.

If I assume that all positive circumstances in my life come from God, then I must also logically conclude that all negative experiences impacting my life are His fault. The problem is that too many professing Christians today want to embrace one conclusion and deny the other, for purposes of fitting God into their own preconceptions of who He is and how He works. From my life experiences, this selective logic fails to account for too many unpleasant realities.

A powerful example of this selective perception of events came to light some years ago as a result of an extended bicycle trip undertaken by our church youth group. About thirty high schoolers, including our daughter Amy, set out on a 450-mile trip from Orlando to north Florida and home again. This is a relatively dangerous endeavor because of the cyclists' constantly close proximity with vehicular traffic. Inevitably, a driver forcing his way through traffic collided with one of the group, flinging him some distance through the air, where he landed on the concrete. Fortunately, he was not injured, and the group was able to safely complete its journey home.

Upon recounting events at a dinner subsequent to their return, the perception of nearly all in attendance was that God was directly responsible for this fortuitous event. He had somehow temporarily intervened in the laws of physics for the purpose of ensuring that the young man was not injured in this accident. As with all the other parents, I too was relieved and thankful that he had been spared what could have been a disaster.

However, I suspect that my unspoken thoughts were much different from those of everyone else present. I couldn't help but wonder, if God was in fact responsible for this good news, then was He not also to blame for the death of the young female cyclist who died under the wheels of a semitrailer truck on a similar trip a few years before?

Being a violence survivor, and no doubt representing the minority Christian voice, I chose to interpret neither of those incidents in terms of God's direct impact upon events but, rather, as simply a frightening example of the terribly capricious nature of circumstances in this world. One person had chosen to wear a helmet, the other had not. One was struck from behind by a car, the other fell into the path of a large truck.

Did God love that young boy more than that girl? Would He consciously choose to save one and allow the other to die? I certainly hope not. I am sickened and saddened at the thought of such a senseless tragedy, but I cannot give God credit for the success without indicting Him in the loss, so I now choose to look for explanations beyond His hands-on involvement in many of life's events such as this one.

In essence, I interpret God's role in worldly circumstances as a double-edged sword that cuts two ways. If I give Him credit for every positive experience, circumstance, or event that affects my life, then I must also (consciously or not) spend the rest of my life looking back over my shoulder and conclude that He was also responsible for the events surrounding my mother's death.

This is not to say that I believe He cannot, or does not, in some instances, through motives and means known only to Him, directly exert His will over physical events taking place in this world. The Bible is filled with accounts to substantiate His abilities in this respect. I just remain very skeptical of claims that His goodness is responsible for every fortunate, albeit unlikely, event or circumstance we may experience.

Perhaps my feelings in this respect were best verbalized by Terry Bowden, former coach of the Auburn University football team in a recent interview. Reflecting on his unexpected success in his first season at Auburn, he stated, "When you go 11-0, you don't know why sometimes. Something steps in and affects your season, and all the little things that win a ball game go your way. I don't have to think that God stepped in and made our season go 11-0, because then I would have to almost say that when we went 6-5, God stepped in and punished us.[4]

My reality as a survivor leads me to believe that the Lord's true power in this world is represented in His ability to influence the hearts and minds of those committing themselves to His will. Thus, I believe His orchestration of events is more realistically a function of millions of independent actions undertaken daily by each of us as believers attempting to carry out His desire in our individual lives.

Those who believe as I do see the most powerful actions of God in a much less discernible, but infinitely more influential, form than any tangible force He may utilize to temporarily disrupt the physical activities of our world to meet a particular purpose. The idealistic part of my nature still wants to believe that God can shape events to meet my individual needs. That same part of me still clings to the lifelong tendency to pray for His intervention in circumstances for the sake of my perceived needs or wants.

However, the battered and bruised violence survivor in me recognizes that the best hope for the Lord's impact on my life now lies within my faithful reliance on Him. I believe I should ask for His help in learning to live with the realities of my circumstances, rather than expecting Him to orchestrate events to conform to my personal interests. Therefore, with this as a focus, I must not ask, "What is God's role in my current reality?" but, rather, "How can I learn to rely on Him to cope with this reality?"

In explaining his perspective of God's role in our lives, Terry Bowden again expressed views, which I interpret as being similar to mine: "I believe that God just gives us a great ability, through our belief in Him, to deal with our situations. That's the only miracle I ever ask God for in my life. I don't pray so much that He change the events of my life, but that He help me deal with the events that would happen in His perfect plan... You begin to think you can do everything on your own. You can't.[5]

I believe that other insights into this issue may be gained from again considering Viktor Frankl's observations regarding his experiences in the Nazi concentration camps. He maintains that while we cannot always control our lives' circumstances, we have unlimited control over how we will choose to react to these circumstances. Our freedom to react, he contends, represents the last of man's freedoms. This freedom of choice is what separates mankind from all order of life on earth.

Additionally, he contends that we are also accountable for our response to circumstances—that we must accept responsibility for how we choose to deal with our existing realities.[6] I believe it is this absence of personal responsibility for our actions of which he speaks that has led to the general decline of ethics and the increase in violence that we are experiencing within contemporary society.

In a Christian context, relative to my own loss through violence, I interpret his precepts to mean that lasting emotional and spiritual health for all survivors can only come once we have accepted this new realization. We must then make the commitment to begin living with this reality as constructively as possible.

As humans enjoying the privilege of free will, we have the option of continuing to rail against fate, to blame God for His acts or omissions, to view the world from a bitter and resentful perspective, and ultimately refuse to live within the constraints of our changed lives.

However, we also have the ability to choose another response. We can recognize that we will never again be who we once were because of what we have experienced—that our lives have been irrevocably altered through circumstances beyond our control. We can admit that in many ways our loss represents the death of a part of our former selves, and as such, life as we once knew it can never be the same. We can learn to accept that whatever else the past may have been, it is forever gone and will exist for us from now on only in our minds in the form of memories. Further, we can recognize that we are actually undergoing a process of not only redefining what we believe, but also reexamining and redefining the nature of our relationship with both our world and our God. Finally, we can concede that the ultimate nature of these relationships will eventually be determined by how we choose to respond to those circumstances that have redirected the remaining course of our lives.

CHAPTER 9

LEARNING TO ACCEPT A
LIFE WITHOUT CLOSURE

For now we see in a mirror dimly, but then face to face.
Now I know in part; then I shall understand fully...

—1 Corinthians 13:12

I have never been one to handle ambiguity very graciously. Because of this, the tormenting questions that surround Mother's death represent at times an almost-insurmountable obstacle to my recovery process. Prior to her murder, I had always maintained a very dichotomous perspective of the world around me. Things were either black or white, good or bad, right or wrong, open or closed. Suddenly, those vague, undefined uncertainties of life that had always been so threatening to me became my constant companion.

I can remember distinctly, early on in the course of events in her case, praying for some closure or resolution. I frequently reminded God that I was the last person in the world who could live with such questions. I reiterated to Him that to be forced to live without knowing what happened or why it happened would be a life sentence of emotional hell for me. I hoped that He would consider this as He went about working things out on my behalf. I have since reached the conclusion, however, that His perspective of my "right" to closure and mine are somewhat different.

I have finally concluded that in our humanity, many of us act as if we enjoy a certain inalienable right to answers to all of our questions. Understandably, those of us dealing with questions left open in the wake of violence feel a tremendous need to experience closure in these issues. I believe that gaining an acceptance of our inability to solve some of our most troubling mysteries represents another significant hurdle all survivors must clear if we ever hope to regain emotional stability.

In an effort to get beyond my own "Why me?" survivor mentality, I have tried to objectively examine all nature of life's tragedies and the many unanswered questions that are often left in their wake. In so doing, I have learned that many other people are forced to live with uncertainty in diverse types of adversity other than mine. Illnesses, economic and financial apprehension, questionable employment status, and doubtful relationships are just a few of the agonizing uncertainties people deal with daily, sometimes for many years. Thus, I try to remember that living without closure in significant issues is really just another frustrating aspect of being human.

Again, from Ellis's rational-emotive perspective, most of us must admit that knowledge with any degree of certainty in this world is by far the exception rather than the rule. To state that mankind might know 1 percent of the fathomless amount of knowledge constituting this universe is probably wildly optimistic. We must therefore recognize that we will never comprehend the vast majority of the mysteries surrounding us. As such, any obsession we may have with obtaining answers to incomprehensible questions represents futility.

I can think of innumerable questions of nominal importance that I live with every day. How does a goose manage to navigate a thousand miles to the same winter nesting ground every year with no external navigational aids? How does the earth continue in its same orbital rotation around the sun after several billion years? How does the process of nuclear fission work on the atomic level? While these questions are discernable for many people, they remain a mystery to me.

Other questions of far greater significance, however, are unanswerable by anyone today and may remain so forever. What actually caused the extinction of the great dinosaurs? What secrets lie unearthed in the aftermath of natural calamities that have assailed this earth for millions of years? By what cosmic forces did God will the universe into existence from once black nothingness? When it comes to issues of such huge proportion, I suspect we know far less than we might want to admit.

Still, as enigmatic as these questions may be, their impact upon us is relatively distant and impersonal. We tend not to dwell on them as ongoing issues of concern.

Those circumstances that impact us personally, however, take on much more importance to us. The point of great significance here, I believe, is that wherever our own vested interests are concerned, the significance we place upon unanswered questions increases tremendously.

Consider the tragedies so common to our world today. Malaysia Air flight 370 mysteriously disappears over the South China Sea en route from Kuala Lumpur to Beijing. Despite thousands of hours of search and recovery efforts since, only a handful of wreckage has been recovered with no sign of any passengers. We can only imagine the anguish their friends and loved ones feel, having no idea what caused their deaths or how the last few moments of their lives played out.[1]

An Amtrak train speeding across an Alabama swamp plunges into a bayou, a number of passengers are killed. Are the survivors of these victims not haunted by speculation on what their loved ones endured in their last moments on earth?

A husband is told by police that his wife died after her car smashed into a tree, and no cause can be determined because there were no witnesses. How many sleepless nights does he endure, wondering what could have caused this? In our humanity, lack of closure in such tragedies is terribly threatening.

Consider also the circumstances surrounding the carnage of combat. Due to its savage nature, lives may be lost under such horrible circumstances that even those surviving may be unable to determine exactly what led to the death of any particular individual.

Retired general Harold Moore describes the slaughter involved in the battle of the la Drang Valley early in the Vietnam War. He states that the American troops fought with such valor that many of the dead should probably have received the Congressional Medal of Honor. Still, there were so few survivors in some units that no one could give an accurate accounting of who actually did what.[2]

He chronicled how most of the surviving family members of those lost in battle were tormented by not knowing the circumstances surrounding the deaths of their loved ones. He described how grateful those survivors were, twenty years later, for any bits and pieces of information that he or others could provide regarding their unsettling concerns.

In reading his story, I had to admit to myself that we survivors are not unique in our battles with unresolved questions.

Even in instances where death may not be at issue, there are countless cases in which people live lifetimes affected by illness or other adversity without any explanation for their circumstances. I think of our one time pastor's daughter, Shawn, who at the age of twelve was stricken by some mysterious illness that unexpectedly denied her the use of her legs. Countless tests were run to determine the reason for her condition, none of which could identify a cause. Years later, she and her family still have no clue as to what caused her debilitation, and she will probably be forced to walk with braces for the rest of her life.

Just as I have prayed repeatedly for relief from my own questions, her father admitted to me that his similar requests for enlightenment have remained for years without answer. While the objective side of me recognizes the fact that these needless hardships are a frequent fact of life, I still find it emotionally very hard to accept such cruel realities as Shawn's without the benefit of some reason why they exist.

A fundamental tenet of the Christian faith, and one that separates Christianity from all other world religions, is our belief that the God of this universe is a personal god. He is not merely some abstract cosmic entity of all-goodness but a personal God who feels a love for each individual and desires a living, personal relationship with each of us. This was obviously the purpose for Christ's incarnation and inevitable death at the hands of this world. Since He is today no longer physically with us, the lifeline by which we maintain this personal relationship with Him remains the act of prayer.

The fact that prayer is the cornerstone of our faith is the reason why it has become the focus of one of the greatest struggles of my own Christian faith. The paradox, as I see it, lies in the fact that the prayer process, which I rely so heavily upon in all aspects of my life, has yet to provide me with the peace of mind attainable only in the resolution of my questions.

If I believed that God did not have the answers I seek, there would be no implication upon my faith. I could simply resign myself to the fact that what I seek is beyond attainment. However, I struggle with the fact that He certainly does have this knowledge and could easily provide me with it if He chose to do so.

My interaction with other victims leads me to believe that I am not alone in expressing this concern. I believe that other Christian survivors may be thinking, if not asking, these same questions. We recognize that our most sincere, heartfelt, and imperative requests of God remain unrequited. In spite of this, we attempt to sustain an unfaltering faith in that same prayer process that preserves our personal relationship with Him.

Certainly, all believers in the power of prayer have had occasions where their requests seemingly went unanswered. So, questions of faith surrounding the value of prayer are not unique to the victims of violence. However, I would suggest that by the very nature of their extremely tragic circumstances, many victims find themselves at some point along the road to recovery seriously re-assessing their feelings about the merits of prayer and its perceived impact upon their lives.

I believe the word of operative significance here may in fact be *perception*. The way we perceive prayer, both in terms of its substance and its impact, will for the most part be the sole determinative factor in the value we place upon it. Prayer, by its very nature, is the consummate intangible. I believe we are demonstrating a certain amount of faith by even attempting the act of prayer, since it is in no way anything that can be tangibly seen, felt, or otherwise experienced. Simply, by faith we hold to the belief that we can solicit God's personal presence in our lives through the act of prayer.

Therefore, relative to this act, we conclude that this process has been a success or failure simply by our perception or interpretation of the events that follow. Consider the following examples:

> Scenario #1
> You have been praying for months that God would get you out of your dead-end job into a more suitable alternative. Result: You finally get a new opportunity with another company. Possible conclusion: God answered your prayer by directly shaping events to create this opportunity for you.

> Scenario #2
> After your wife is diagnosed with inoperable cancer and given only a short time to live, you pray repeatedly that she be healed and spared a premature death. Result: She dies within six months. Possible conclusion: God decided not to intervene on her behalf and thus allowed her to die.

The problem in attempting to assess the efficacy of prayer lies in the fact that none of us as humans has enough facts to draw any accurate conclusions. Only God, through His infinite wisdom, can accurately say how and why any prayer is answered. We can only make educated guesses based on how we perceive subsequent events to unfold.

Our expectation of prayer relative to its outcome thus becomes the determinant factor in our assessment of its results. We perceive a particular need in our lives and take this to God through prayer, in the belief that He can assist us.

We come to Him, however, in most cases, with some expectation of specifically what He should be doing for us. That is, we may unknowingly dictate terms for how He should respond to our requests.

Relative to my mother's case, I have always felt that my pleas for closure and justice were both reasonable and achievable for a God as powerful as mine. A part of me still continues to expect Him to figure out some way for me to obtain closure in her death. Yet, for some reason known only to Him, my repeated requests for His assistance in this issue have to date remained without answer.

My expectation continues to be that He provide the answers I need. Thus, the failure to obtain this knowledge means that my prayer has been in vain from the narrow perspective of my own human expectations. Beyond this, however, I cannot accurately determine whether my prayers have been successful or not because I do not have a viewpoint that is broad enough to discern all the possible implications.

I suppose such perceived lack of response to my prayers could be interpreted from any number of positions. During that period when anger, bitterness, and resentment consumed my existence, it was easy for me to believe that God had simply chosen to ignore my requests, and thus attribute this silence to His lack of concern for my feelings. This simplistic, *and* erroneous, view of God fit well with my distorted perspective of the world at that time.

Others might interpret these same circumstances as a lack of faith on my part. Some probably believe that my requests were denied because God in His wisdom knew that I doubted, even if subconsciously, that He would act on my behalf. They would say His failure to assist me, then, was to some degree my own fault.

Another explanation that I have heard in circumstances similar to mine is that we are sometimes better off without some knowledge, because it could be too horrible to accept. While I appreciate such an empathetic interpretation, in the case of a person such as myself, any answer, no matter how terrible, is preferable to the prolonged torment of uncertainty.

I could also choose the optimistic interpretation that God will eventually reveal to me at least the answers I seek, and perhaps in time, even allow me to see justice served. My old police nature, however, prevents me from embracing this position. I know of too many instances in which other survivors die without ever receiving the closure so critical to their recovery process.

For instance, one of the most notorious murders ever recorded still remains unsolved today, almost 70 years after its occurrence. The case of the Black Dahlia first came to the attention of Los Angeles police in the late 1940s. This murder was particularly bizarre and heinous because the victim had been surgically dissected by her murderer. Her limbs and her head had been severed with great skill and placed adjacent to her body, perhaps indicating the work of a trained medical professional.

Police remained throughout this time without a motive or probable perpetrator. Initially, the only means they had for identifying her body was through a black tattoo of a dahlia flower on her shoulder, by which they began to refer to the victim as "the Black Dahlia." They ultimately identified her as Elizabeth Short and concluded that she had probably been a street person who had stumbled upon the wrong person and was murdered without apparent reason. It is highly unlikely that this case will ever be solved after the passage of so much time.[3]

The Lord alone knows the anguish experienced by her surviving family and friends. Did they live out their days wondering what had happened to their sister, daughter, or loved one? Did they turn to God for answers that they were denied, just as mine have been? Did their faith suffer or die as a result of their bitter disappointment?

Compounding the difficulty in our quest for closure in cases of violence is the fact that even the perpetrators of violence themselves are often without conscious knowledge of their true motives. Certainly, most any violent sociopath could give you some superficial reason for his actions: he didn't like what someone said, she was too flirtatious and seductive, the victim "asked for it."

These are only surface motives, however, because the real answers require explaining why anyone would choose to operate so far beyond the normal boundaries of societal and self-restraint. Those who elect to rape, terrorize, or murder another human being are often pursuing psychological drives that are deeply ingrained in their subconscious. This reality in no way mitigates their despicable deeds or absolves them of full responsibility for their actions. Still, the foot fetishist, the child molester, and the serial murderer are all usually reacting to some experience that happened so early in their lives that they may not even consciously remember the incident. Therefore, in most cases, a victim such as myself would be unable to literally beat the reasons for their behavior out of these depraved creatures.

In the aftermath of Mother's murder, I have reached the sad and frightening conclusion that we live in such a sick world where innocent people are slaughtered or otherwise victimized simply because a repugnant element of society enjoys committing these acts. Concluding that my mother's life ended for nothing more than the repulsive pleasure of some faceless demon is probably as close to the truth surrounding her death as I will ever get. And as much as I detest this reality, there is nothing I can do to change it.

Interestingly, as I have attempted to explain my frustrating doubts of faith regarding prayer and God's role in our lives, nowhere in the Bible have I found Him to explain, justify, or apologize for His actions. In fact, in the book of Isaiah, He states, "For my thoughts are not your thoughts, neither are your ways my ways… For as the heavens are higher than the earth, so are my ways higher than your ways and my thoughts than your thoughts" (Isa. 55:8-9).

Throughout all of Job's travails, and even after God restored his life, at no time did God explain why He permitted Job to suffer so terribly. In fact, God's only response was to confront Job's questions by reminding him that as Creator of the world who set in motion all our natural forces, He was under no obligation to explain His actions to Job or anyone else (Job 38-41).

Reading Psalms reiterates the fact that God is not One to offer explanations to man. As David was pursued relentlessly by Saul, intent on literally having his head, David poignantly expressed his bewilderment at why the righteous are often forced to suffer and die at the hands of the wicked. Again, God neither intervened in David's circumstances nor offered any explanations or apologies.

As I interpret these scriptures, I perceive His role under such conditions more as that of compassionate and empathetic listener, rather than as the great cosmic technician intervening in events for our favor. I believe He is deeply concerned about our circumstances and emotional struggles and is willing to share, but not eliminate, these terrible burdens. While I often wish that He would rescue me from my distress, my interpretation of the Bible says that such an expectation may be unrealistic.

I believe Dr. James Dobson best captures my feelings on the issue of God's enigmatic ways when he states, "He has never made Himself accountable to man, nor will He ever. He will not be cross-examined or interrogated. Nowhere in the Bible does God speak defensively or seek our approval on His actions. He simply says, 'Trust me.'⁴"

Obviously, in attempting to address such a profound issue as why prayers appear to go unanswered, there are probably as many interpretations as there are believing Christians. In my own examination of this subject, I have certainly gained no infinite wisdom in this matter. I have, however, come to believe that there may be many mitigating factors involved, not the least of which include my perspective of worldly events and my expectations of God.

Thus, I can only conclude that many of the answers I seek lie within that unlimited storehouse of knowledge that will remain known only to God. Therefore, for the sake of maintaining my faith, I have decided that we sometimes must simply resign ourselves to let God be God in how He responds to our requests, whether we like it or not.

Only He knows how I have resisted conceding the struggle to find some reason for my mother's death. Only He knows how badly it hurts to admit that in all probability, I will die without ever knowing the circumstances surrounding the terrible fate that ended her life. Only He knows how many times I have doubted His concern for me as I have puzzled over His continued silence in this matter.

However, as much as I may resent it in my own humanity, as much as I may disagree with His decision to not provide me those answers I seek, I am trying to learn to make my faith in Him stronger than my doubts about the way He works in my life. While a part of me still believes it is inherently unfair to all of us who constantly seek those answers that only He holds, I recognize that continuing to rely on Him in spite of these misgivings is a demonstration of faith that I might not be able to achieve through any other circumstances.

And although I can never envision myself coming to like the reality of living the remainder of my life without closure, I do hope that through a continuing reliance upon Him, I can eventually come to accept it.

CHAPTER 10

JUSTICE WILL PREVAIL... BUT NOT THIS SIDE OF ETERNITY

For we must all appear before the judgment seat of Christ,
so that each one may receive good or evil,
according to what he has done in the body.

—2 Corinthians 5:10

Webster's Basic English Dictionary defines justice as "just or right action or treatment... the quality of being fair or just." The Bible states that "the Almighty will not pervert justice" (Job 34:12) and that "the Lord... does no wrong" (Zeph. 3:5). I am aware of no ideal that is loftier than that embodied in the concept of true justice, and the Lord God is the quintessential example of living fairness and justice. The disparity, however, between justice as evidenced in God Himself and its application in our spiritually bankrupt world today represents perhaps the last and greatest threat to my own hope for recovery as a violence survivor.

I do acknowledge that God and His perfect justice will ultimately prevail over this world. However, the war between good and evil, right and wrong, justice and injustice will continue to claim countless casualties until He decides to intervene for our sake at the final judgment.

We who are the victims of this temporal struggle between good and evil no longer ask ourselves whether we will be victimized by it. Instead, we now search for answers as to how we will live with its dreadful realities without sacrificing our sanity or faith in the process.

Abandoning my expectation that justice must prevail has been my most difficult concession resulting from Mother's death. Early in childhood, I believe, I subconsciously began forming my paradigm of the world through which I perceived that good must somehow triumph over evil. Because right was right and wrong was wrong, God must be on the side of those who practiced what was right and good.

Through all the ensuing years, I waded through life clutching tenaciously in my mind to the banner of "fairness" and "justice" that I held to be everyone's birthright. Even when I witnessed the nightmarish perversions of justice so familiar to those in law enforcement, I still refused to let this flag fall into the sewer of worldly travesty and be swept away along with so many other lost ideals. Finally, however, my last bastion of idealism died along with my mother on that fateful night in January.

In contrasting my current view of the world with my perspective of years past, I now see that the Christian precepts of fair play, honesty, good faith, and respect for others, inherent in the concept of God's justice, rest on a crumbling earthly foundation. Christ Himself embodied all that was good, noble, and right, and yet was put to death by the very forces of greed, envy, selfishness, and hatred that He came to destroy. He did, in fact, prevail over these with His resurrection after death, and He will do so again with His incarnation at the final judgment. Nevertheless, those of us struggling to survive in this inherently wicked world remain just as subject to the consequences of these deadly forces today, as He was then.

I am beginning to accept that justice, as we experience it in this world, and justice in the eyes of God the Almighty bear no resemblance to each other. The fact is that *moral relativism* and *situational ethics*, are undermining all nature of our relationships. The fact is that greed and avarice have become the predominant forces driving world commerce today. The fact is that our criminal "justice" system has been subverted by the moral decline of this country, which threatens the survival of both. The fact is that sin dominates this world, and suffering on an unimaginable scale takes place as a result.

All of which lead me to conclude that the principles of justice and fairness which are intended in God's sight to govern man's relationships with other men, have long since given way to the practices of selfishness and contempt for others that dominate our contemporary world.

Still, until we are victimized directly, most of us, and particularly practicing Christians, tend to approach life with a Pollyanna-type mentality that refuses to recognize the magnitude of worldly corruption and spiritual decay surrounding us all. We see the never-ending tale of misery played out on the evening news, we read every day in the newspaper the sordid details of evil carrying out its vile mission, our daily commute to work allows us to hear the particulars of hatred that played themselves out during the course of the previous night. Yet many of us remain untouched at the heart level by the injustices everywhere around us.

Even as the skeptical and pessimistic ex-cop, I continued to find ways, prior to my mother's death, to selectively filter out much of the world's cruel realities. My own ideals of fairness, goodness, and justice were so strongly ingrained that I believed these to be entitlements available to everyone. I felt certain that God would somehow ultimately preserve these, inviolate, even in this corrupt world.

Now that I have personally experienced the bitter fruits of violence and evil, I will probably spend the remainder of my life resisting the urge to succumb to despair and hopelessness over the condition of our world. Ample cause certainly exists to give up on the worldly state of affairs if we wanted to. Any sense of responsibility and accountability for one's actions in our society is almost nonexistent. The practice of honesty and fairness in our dealings with others has been forgotten by all but a few. Respect for life is at a historic low, as evidenced in the current rates of abortion and murder.

The bitter and cynical part of my nature, like a sponge, absorbs the data to support such a fatalistic view of the world. I see directors of charities, leaders in churches, and executives of businesses robbing their constituents blind to support their greed and avarice. Professional athletes hold their fans ransom in demand for outrageous salaries, while rock musicians insult our sensitivities or indulge in perverted activities like child molestation. Few politicians today can be trusted to do anything they promise, and more and more are being indicted for crimes ranging from misappropriation of funds to child pornography. A frightening number of law enforcement personnel have capitulated to temptation and sacrificed their honor on the altar of bloody drug money. Many of today's college students admit that they routinely cheat on exams and have no sense of obligation to do otherwise. Criminals commit heinous crimes, only to receive trivial sentences or "walk the charges" entirely after being found innocent.

Even worse, each year in this country, more than 1,000 convicted murderers; 7,000 convicted rapists; and 36,000 people convicted of aggravated assault will not go to prison.[1] For those who are incarcerated, punishment is anything but just. The average time convicted felons in this country spend in prison is 8.7 years for murder, 5.2 years for rape, 3.8 years for robbery, and 2.2 years for aggravated assault.[2] Where is God's justice in all of this?

Nowhere have I heard other survivors more angry than when voicing their bitterness and resentment at the injustices they have all been subjected to. After enduring the torment of endless police investigations, countless court delays and continuances, the circus-like tactics of defense lawyers sitting next to smirking defendants, some may eventually see "justice" served years later in the form of token sentences meted out to the guilty. These illustrations do not even address the huge number of crimes that never go to court because of plea bargains negotiated, the number of criminals who are convicted of lesser crimes, or the number of convictions resulting only in probation or community diversion programs for the offender.

Then there are those instances in which obviously guilty perpetrators of crimes never stand trial for their offenses. Usually this results when circumstantial evidence (defined as any case lacking eyewitnesses or forensic evidence) is strong enough to indicate a prime suspect, but insufficient to justify an arrest. Nearly all law enforcement investigators can easily recall cases in which they are certain that a particular individual is responsible for a crime. Nevertheless, they were unable to make an arrest because the legal burden of proof against the accused could not be overcome in a court of law. This circumstance is frustrating for police and infuriating for surviving family and friends.

An example of such a case involves my friend Corinne, whom I know through her active involvement in the Parents of Murdered Children organization. Her son was brutally murdered a number of years ago. Both the Garden City, Kansas, police investigators and Corinne's family feel certain that they know who committed the murder, as well as why he did it. Sadly, despite overwhelming evidence of his guilt, this suspect was eventually tried and subsequently acquitted. Just one more example of justice miscarried

For those cases that do go to court, the proceedings often take on the appearance of a legal charade, where everyone but the defendant appears to be on trial. Whenever a criminal is obviously guilty, his/her lawyer will invariably begin to construct a defense based upon impugnment of the victim or witness. Their rationale for this course of action is simple desperation. If there were any possible doubt as to the guilt of an accused, they would pursue legitimate avenues of defense. Since this isn't possible, all they can do is mount an attack on the character of the innocent.

What I believe to be one of the most blatant examples of this mockery of justice is evidenced in a well-publicized 1970s murder trial. A socially prominent and very wealthy Ft. Worth oilman had married a woman with whom he had little in common. Marital problems between the two ensued shortly after the marriage, and she eventually filed for divorce. During the separation period, he was ordered by court decree to vacate the premises, leaving her in the couple's multimillion-dollar mansion.

He was shortly thereafter arrested and accused of murdering both his estranged wife's lover and her daughter in their residence. Being in law enforcement and involved in part of the security role we assumed for her during this time, I was able to hear her candid comments on exactly how the crime took place.

She stated that he had entered her residence in her absence, dressed as a burglar. During which time, she contended, he shot and killed her daughter.

When she later arrived to find him standing over her daughter's body, she stated that he simply said "Hi," and then shot both her and her boyfriend. While he reportedly stood over her male companion and fired another round into his body, she was able to escape, despite her injuries, and call the police. He later stood trial for murder and attempted murder.

Ultimately, having the benefit of a nationally renowned defense attorney, he was acquitted based largely upon his lawyer's ability to discredit her testimony in court. As an eyewitness, she had actually observed her friend's murder and her own attempted murder. Nevertheless, the defense was able to use her questionable lifestyle as a diversion to deflect the question of guilt away from his client.

More and more today, we see criminal defendants using other ludicrous defenses to absolve themselves of responsibility for their actions. Damian Monroe Williams and Henry Keith Watson, accused of violent criminal activities during the Los Angeles riots, received only nominal sentences after claiming a lack of responsibility for their actions. Their attorney contended that they had been motivated by "justifiable rage" and had succumbed to a "mob mentality.[3]"

Of course, there has always been the catch-all of legal defenses: "temporary insanity." But now it is being used with increasing frequency to justify outlandish crimes. I fail to understand how one can be sane immediately prior to and after the murder or injury of another, but suffer some temporary lapse of "sanity" during the commission of a crime.

The specious "victim of abuse" defense was used in the notorious case of the Menendez brothers who brutally murdered both of their parents with sixteen rounds from a shotgun. Despite overwhelming evidence against them, including their verbal confessions, it took three trials to finally get a jury to see beyond their bogus sexual abuse defense and declare both guilty of murder.[4]

In this same context, I am hearing with increasing frequency the term "irresistible urge," utilized by defendants to justify their murderous actions. Under this rationale, one can state that he was overwhelmed by the irresistible urge to commit an act of violence against another (usually because the victim allegedly created such intolerable conditions) and claim that because of these circumstances, he has no culpability for the crime.

My interpretation of God's standard of justice is that under no circumstance (except, perhaps, the rare instances of clinical insanity—which is neither temporary nor curable), are we absolved of responsibility for our every action. I refuse to accept the world's compromised standard of accountability, which maintains that some circumstances are so overwhelming that we, like animals, are justified in succumbing to these "irresistible urges."

Cases such as these illustrate what I believe to be one of the crudest miscarriages of justice inflicted upon victims in this day and age. This is the despicable tactic of turning the victim into the perceived criminal and the criminal into the perceived victim, sometimes referred to as "victimology."[5]

With increasing frequency, criminals are escaping true justice at the expense of their victims who are depicted in the media and courtrooms as the real offenders. This is even more abhorrent when the victims have been murdered and have no day in court to defend themselves by revealing the truth.

In essence, victims today are often victimized twice: through their initial injury or death, then once again through impugnment of their names, reputations, and honor. Where is God's justice when the good names of decent people are being dragged through the sewer by money-hungry demagogues?

The consequences of prison experienced by many criminals who are incarcerated for their crimes heap further indignities upon our justice system. I read in near disbelief recently the words of one prison guard (written anonymously for fear of reprisal) as he described the "punishment" received by inmates in the Ohio prison system. He detailed the privileges enjoyed by inmates in a maximum-security facility. These included a health center complete with weight and exercise machines, newly constructed, state-of-the-art facilities for each of the sports of baseball, basketball, and football, cable television with the Playboy channel, picnics and pizza dinners once a month for all inmates, tuition-free college education, and access to a comprehensive legal library (which many inmates utilized to bring suit against the state for "grievances"). All these privileges were, of course, paid for by the citizens of the state of Ohio, many of whom were in fact the victims of those they are now supporting!

He went on to add that guards had been instructed to use no physical force against inmates under any circumstances—a policy that had recently led to the death of one guard. Further, guards had been instructed to take no retaliatory effort against inmates should prisoners commit such routine acts as throwing urine or feces at them. Instead, guards were to inquire what it was they might have done to provoke such an outburst in order to avoid doing it in the future.[6] I wonder, is this how God envisioned our administration of His justice?

Instances like these are why many bitter survivors and cynical law enforcement personnel refer to this as the "criminal injustice system" or the "criminal's justice system." All too often, it is just that.

A survey conducted a few years ago substantiated the distrust felt by much of the public toward our legal system. This data indicated that nearly half of the respondents believed that the defendants are treated better than victims in criminal cases. More than half expressed the opinion that judicial sentencing practices are too lenient. These same respondents also advocated significant changes in the system, including the use of victim impact statements, ensuring financial compensation for victims and the prevention of criminals profiting from their crimes through books and films.[7]

I believe any responsible citizen should be incensed at these perversions of justice. In effect, these societal malefactors thumb their noses at their victims, their victims' survivors, and all of society in general. The likelihood of justice being achieved in their cases is the farthest thing from their minds as they continue to smirk at society in their arrogance and impunity.

The following quote is often attributed to King Solomon, but I can find no biblical confirmation of this, so I will leave the source anonymous. In any event, I believe this statement is very powerful and most applicable to today's society, "Justice will only be achieved when those who are not injured by crime feel as indignant as those who are."

My feelings in this respect were stated most recently in an article by Dr. Dobson, where he writes,

> The way justice is dispensed in a society is a function of its basic moral values, especially in a government of the people, for the people, and by the people. If the majority of its citizens understand and are committed to fundamental principles of right and wrong—based on the Ten Commandments and what has been called 'The natural law of God'—then their judges and juries will render decisions based on those values. But, if the people become confused about what they believe, then their legal apparatus will also lose its focus. It stands to reason, doesn't it? A system of justice can be no better than the value system it represents."[8]

I am convinced that our justice system lies in critical moral condition. I truly believe that our entire legal process is in very real jeopardy of collapsing under the weight of years of moral decay, ethical decline, and blatant exploitation. I feel strongly that society must soon wake up to the fact that we survivors have known for years—that we are all ultimately victimized when justice takes the form of criminals' "rights" prevailing over the legitimate rights of innocent victims.

The fact that a democracy is the least restrictive form of government in the world is, ironically, why it is the most tenuous and subject to its own destruction. A free form of government can last only as long as those within society respect what it represents and willingly abide by its precepts. Once a significantly large element of society chooses to abuse this privilege of freedom, the total collapse of the system itself cannot be far behind.

From a societal perspective, every time one person is victimized, we are all victimized. Every act of dishonesty, every threatened use of force, every act of intimidation, every injury, every robbery, every rape, and every murder diminishes us all to some degree. Each single act of violence repeated thousands of times every day cheapens the value of life, degrades our society, undermines our legal system, and makes this world a more dangerous place in which to live. Our expectations of life decline proportionately as the level of evil and violence escalates around us. The cost of this carnage is immeasurable from every conceivable perspective: physical, financial, emotional, and spiritual.

Now that I am at the point in my recovery process where I have begun to rationally address the full implication of these injustices for what they are, I am trying to accept them at a heart level. Unfortunately, intellectually recognizing that the devil and his evil rule this world still has limited impact upon my ability to incorporate the consequences of this reality into my Christian faith.

I still battle every day with the urge to blame God for this sordid state of affairs, for not intervening for the sake of every person in this world who has to live with the frustration of injustice. I have to fight the impulse to lash out every time I see justice mocked, the guilty shaking their fists in the face of both society and God, daring either to stop them. I want to appoint myself minister of justice and personally see to it that they get what they deserve.

Every time I hear a survivor's tale of tragedy, I battle for the self-control to keep from demanding of God that He do something to stop this madness. As I review this never-ending parade of outrage, I ask myself how long He will permit this savagery to continue without retribution. Each day that passes without me seeing the one who murdered my mother brought to account for his actions represents another test of my faith in the ultimate wisdom of God to do what is right in His own timing.

However, despite the intensity of these emotions, I am coming to recognize that, once again, my perspective has a very great influence upon how I react to these circumstances and incorporate their consequences into my faith. If I choose to focus solely on the magnitude of injustice in this world, if my perspective revolves only around what this evil has done to my life, then I must eventually succumb to bitterness and despair. The overwhelming magnitude of evil in this world and its devastating consequences in countless lives is truly enough to drive a believer from a solid faith in God to a sense of hopelessness and abandonment of faith. Therefore, I again must concede that my own mental health and the survival of my faith rests largely upon my ability to adopt a broader perspective of life, circumstances, and God's role in them all.

To this end, my good friend and counselor, Russ, with whom I have shared many discussions on this subject, has made me aware of a crucial insight. He has considerable experience counseling many of those who represent the violent element of society. I am now coming to share his belief that the people who spend their lifetimes destroying others, ironically, end up serving some form of justice upon themselves as a result of their evil actions. The point he makes is that much of the pain and suffering these evildoers inflict upon others eventually comes back to haunt them in the form of imprisonment in a lifestyle that most of us would consider intolerable.

This critical observation has helped me in moving beyond my obsession with the lack of justice in this world. I am slowly coming to recognize that those who habitually practice evil and inflict pain and suffering upon others live with a set of consequences unique to their own exploitative and predatory way of life. Because of the fact that their world revolves around dominance, control, and abuse of others, they must always face a future of emptiness, mistrust, and fear.

These perpetrators of violence, by their very existence, deny themselves any possibility of experiencing a satisfying life. Not only do they have no faith in God, they can enjoy no lasting, meaningful relationships with anyone around them because their sole concern lies in ensuring their own survival. They isolate themselves from the very elements of life—a satisfying family relationship and a lasting faith in God—that most of us would consider essential to our happiness and success in life. Effectively, they as much as sentence themselves to a life of hell on earth in the form of a fearful, empty, and hopeless existence. They are like emotional black holes—cold and distant, emotionally isolated from everyone around them, and representing a tremendous danger to anyone who happens to get too close.

Granted, this is often very hard to confirm through casual observation. The drug kingpin who enjoys a luxurious lifestyle, complete with his own harem of beautiful women; the Mafia don who drives a Ferrari and owns the multimillion-dollar estate overlooking the Pacific; the murderer who walks out of court acquitted of his heinous crime; and a smiling Bashar al-Assad waving at his legions after gassing hundreds of innocent citizens, would all seem to belie this fact.

I still believe, however, that beneath their veneer of happiness and success lies a rotting core of abject human corruption. These people represent the consummate waste of humanity. Though they would never admit it to anyone, they recognize that they are devoid of all those human feelings that ultimately give any meaning to life. Despite all outward appearances, they live in prisons of their own making. They are doomed to a predatory, animal-like existence, dominated by an unending effort to stay one step ahead of their enemies or evade the police. They will spend the rest of their lives looking over their shoulders and sleeping with one eye open, hoping that their unspeakable acts don't somehow eventually catch up with them.

Deep down inside, beneath all my own pain, grief, anger, and obsession for revenge, I know that the person who murdered my mother will actually end up victimizing himself as much as he has me. I know that his sole motivation for living will continue to be stalking, terrorizing, and murdering other defenseless women. His entire, pathetic existence in this world will be consumed with exerting power and control over the innocent, inflicting pain and destruction upon those around him, destroying everything he touches. And this perverted thirst can never be quenched.

For the remainder of his miserable life, he will run from himself and others on an endless treadmill of fantasy fulfillment. His entire life's energies will be consumed by his obsession with conquering just one more victim, committing that error-free crime, outwitting the police, fulfilling that murderous fantasy that is the only sexual outlet he has, all in a pitiful attempt to justify to others, but primarily to himself, that he is his own little god—superior to everyone else on earth. And while his despicable, murderous life endeavors will probably continue without recrimination, I know that he will still go to bed every night haunted by demons of his own making—the ghosts of suspicion, fear, envy, self-loathing, and hatred.

While the human side of me still relishes the thought of being able to personally do to him the exact things he did to my mother in the last minutes of her life, the Christian side of me remembers that there is a broader perspective that I must consider. I have to recognize that to do so would make me guilty of the exact same atrocity he is guilty of—playing God—and that I would lower myself to the same bestial plane of existence on which he exists.

I must recognize that if I surrender my life to this obsession for revenge, in so doing, I will be sacrificing my relationship with the Lord, who is my only hope for survival in this world, as well as the next. I must constantly remind myself that while the monster of my nightmares will never answer either to me or the agents of justice in this world, he will indeed ultimately answer to the Supreme Agent of Justice of this universe.

I realize now that this effort to transcend my obsession for revenge and see justice served in this world will be an ongoing effort for the remainder of my life. I also recognize that my success or failure in this respect will be determined largely by my ability to replace my human focus on bitterness and resentment with a broader perspective that focuses on God's ability, and promise, to settle all accounts.

As I heard one survivor in a television interview tearfully state after the murder of her son, "They may escape man's justice, but they can't hide from God's."

In my mind, that grieving mother's words captured the essence of what has become the key to my success in learning to live with the injustices of this world. She unknowingly reminded me that I must force myself to focus on the fact that there will eventually come a day when these practitioners of violence stand before the God of this universe Himself, who will pronounce His own perfect sentence upon them in keeping with what they truly have coming.

At that time, there will be nowhere else for them to hide. Their legacies of lies, exploitation, and abuse will no longer be enough to ensure their survival. Their unending run from justice will be over, and they will have nothing left to face but the consequences. They will be forced to look up into the face of the Creator of all living things, whose eyes will burn with rage at the grief, misery, and suffering they have inflicted upon His people.

Finally, at that instant in eternity, their fates will be sealed, and justice will at last be served.

Just as certainly, I know that the murderer of my mother will himself eventually stand before God's judgment seat to account for his atrocities. At that time, God Himself, who knows the terror of my mother's last moments on earth, the look of incomprehensible disbelief on my daughter's face upon hearing of her grandmother's fate, and the horror my mother's brother experienced as he identified her ravaged body, will render justice. He will remember the unspeakable agony I felt when her death was confirmed, He will see my son sobbing in my wife's arms at Mother's funeral, He will not forget the hell on earth my wife endured as she watched my grief nearly tear me apart, He will understand the hopeless despair that Mother's sisters have lived with since her death. He will remember everything... and we will all be avenged at last.

Therefore, despite all my human resentment at life's unfairness and my anger with God's inexhaustible supply of patience, the lifeline that sustains my faith through all my doubts and misgivings is knowing that, eventually, He will ensure that His justice prevails. I am learning to accept that in His own time, according to His wisdom, in a manner that He determines to be acceptable, He will balance the scales of justice. He will settle all accounts, including mine.

So, the last task of recovery that I face at this point in my life is learning to accept the fact that I must leave the management of the affairs of this world to the God who created it and accept Him at His word when He says, "Vengeance is mine, I will repay" (Rom. 12:19).

CHAPTER 11

THE CONTINUOUS PROCESS OF EMOTIONAL RECOVERY

But they who wait for the Lord shall renew their strength,
they shall mount up with wings like eagles,
they shall run and not be weary, they shall walk and not faint.

—Isaiah 40:31

Time is the great healer of all wounds. At least that is what the overused and trivial adage would have us believe. As one who will spend the remainder of his days recovering from one of life's most devastating circumstances, however, I believe there are certain wounds that time can never completely heal. We can only hope to somehow learn to cope with the painful aftermath, and anticipate a future in which the good days eventually outnumber the bad.

Those of us surviving violence must recognize that our very core selves have been dramatically altered by what we have endured. We eventually have to accept that a large part of who we once were is irretrievably gone forever. It is impossible for us to ever again be who we once were before the violence tore our lives apart. To believe otherwise is like denying the reality of a tornado sweeping away our home, leaving us with just a foundation. What existed before is now gone, and we are forced to rebuild, no matter how much we want to deny it.

I personally know too many survivors who are still wandering around in the midst of their emotional rubble, months or years after the storm, refusing to admit to others, or even themselves, that life as they knew it is gone forever. They continue to go through the motions, denying that sooner or later they must begin the painful process of rebuilding if they are to ever have a chance of regaining control of their lives.

Only the Lord knows how I too have resisted coming to grips with this reality since my mother was killed. He alone knows how many times I have tried to wish it all away, refused to accept that I will be without answers for a lifetime, deluded myself into believing that her killer will be brought to justice, fooled myself into believing it would somehow be her when the phone rang, and reread the articles detailing her death as if their sad conclusions could somehow be altered with the passage of enough time.

In spite of all the changes I have undergone, however, not everything concerning my outlook in life has been altered. A few constants do still remain.

Fortunately, my dad taught me from the time I was a young boy that life was tough, and that only the strongest could expect to survive. As I have found out in struggling to cope with Mother's murder, Dad's assessment was more correct than I could ever have imagined. I believe his determination to instill in me his own results-oriented, make-no-excuses approach to life has been critical to my surviving the horror of violence.

I've always known that predators of the highest order exist among us who would commit any act to ensure gratification of their own selfish needs. I now have a much better understanding of what constitutes these people's nature, however, because I have experienced firsthand the fruits of their labor.

Simply stated, these practitioners of evil represent the quintessential worst of mankind. They are the emotionally rabid carnivores of this world, lying in wait for every opportunity to prey upon the unsuspecting, and then arrogantly rationalizing their despicable deeds at every turn. Little of my outlook on life regarding this element of society has changed.

I was raised to believe that the God of this universe was all powerful, all knowing, and all loving. That conviction has survived my experience with violence, though I still often wonder how He works His will in this world. And while I may not understand much of what He does, I have decided that I cannot allow these doubts to alter my conviction that He still controls this universe, and that He will ultimately right all wrongs.

Despite these few remaining constants, I have been forced to significantly reevaluate most of my value convictions because of what I have endured.

For one, my expectations of life are considerably less demanding now than they were prior to my tragedy. If I live to enjoy good health, financial security, and professional success, I will consider myself fortunate indeed, because nowhere in all of my musings on life have I discovered these to be my inalienable right. The fateful winds of this world blow tragedy, suffering, and despair in every direction; and no one is exempt from assault by these terrible forces.

I have decided that Albert Ellis was right on target when he suggested that most of our emotional maladjustments stem from our unrealistic expectations of life. Though it is probably pessimistic, my unspoken approach to life at this point could probably be described as "expect little from life so you won't be disappointed when life doesn't come through for you."

Accepting this reality has allowed me to concede that I will never see closure in the questions surrounding Mother's death. As unfair as this may be, I can now accept it as my permanent reality. Only through examining my own misfortune in this respect have I been able to recognize, however, that countless others in this world face frustration stemming from questions that are equally crucial to them. Though it still remains a painful process, I am learning to accept that such mysteries represent just a small part of that huge body of knowledge lying outside our realm of human understanding.

Paradoxically because of this belief, whatever fear of death I may once have known is now nonexistent. As a Christian, I have never really been afraid of dying, because I have always maintained a faith that the life for me after this one will be complete and without want. And while I am not eagerly awaiting its arrival, I will have neither fear nor regret when it comes. That is because only through dying can I ever hope to receive the answers to the questions which will always haunt my existence in this world.

At some point in the next world, will all the mysteries surrounding January 18, 1991, be revealed to me? Will I learn everything that happened that night? Will I know who did it, and perhaps understand the convoluted logic he used to justify his atrocity? Will I also have the satisfaction of knowing that whoever took my mother's life will face the eternal consequences of his actions? If God wills it, all this will be revealed to me at that time.

Because justice has eluded my mother's case, and is perverted in so many others, I am resigned now to the fact that true justice in this world can never be attained. Perhaps this is why I relish those rare instances where good does briefly prevail over evil, where those who have it coming receive just payment, or when right overcomes wrong.

Nevertheless, I no longer cling to any false expectation that I will ever see justice ultimately triumph over the evils of this world. If anything, as the clock winds down on mankind, the continued mockery of all decency and fairness will only increase. Therefore, we can all expect to be victimized as a result.

If this conclusion is accurate, however, then disastrous consequences lie ahead for the future of our society. The survival of the freedom we enjoy is a function of the respect we demonstrate for it. When we abdicate this responsibility by allowing the abuses of the lawless element to prevail over the legitimate rights of responsible members of society, we have placed our entire way of life in jeopardy. I honestly believe that the gift of freedom we have so long taken for granted now rests upon a sinking foundation. As such, I cannot see this society surviving far into the future if its violent and criminal factors are allowed to usurp the rights of its honest citizenship much longer.

I have learned something else through the horror of losing my mother that I don't believe I ever completely grasped prior to her death. That is, that love is the most powerful force in the universe, capable of overcoming even the fires of hatred. Speaking as one who has experienced the extreme of both of these emotions, I am convinced that the power of love can transcend anything—even death itself.

By that, I mean that a bond of love, once established between two people, becomes inseparable. The love I enjoyed with my mother and my dad while they were alive was one of the greatest gifts I will ever experience. Though they are gone, I know that they love me still, even though we are separated for a season. And while I can no longer see them or experience their presence, there is no doubt in my mind that their love for me will prevail throughout eternity.

My hope for a reunion, therefore, lies in the future. That is the fuel that keeps me going, even during those times when it would be so much easier to give up.

The fact that I lost my mother to such savage and unexpected circumstances may be the reason why I now place an even higher value on those relationships that mean the most to me. Perhaps it is only through surviving such tragedy that we can ever fully recognize just how fragile and fleeting life is. I realize now only too well that the people and relationships I value most can literally be here today and gone tomorrow. I hope this critical insight will allow me to better appreciate my relationships with my family and friends, never taking them for granted and always cherishing their presence as the greatest of all treasures in my life.

This realization has prompted me to make a commitment to focus more on the present moment. All of us can easily get so caught in the trap of fretting over the past or worrying about the future that we completely lose sight of the value of the present.

My mother warned me for years that my uncompromising drive to accomplish all my goals was jeopardizing my ability to appreciate the many good things surrounding me at the time. Now that she is gone, I believe I have found out the hard way what she meant. She always insisted that I take time to smell the roses, and I hope that for the sake of her memory, I can now learn to better appreciate all those little things that mean so much.

Author and speaker Jim Autry mirrors my feelings in this respect when he reminds us: if we are angry, we are living in the past; if we are fearful, we are living in the future.[1] A critical step down the road to recovery for all victims is learning to find that productive middle ground between our rightful anger at our past circumstances and our understandable anxiety toward our future.

Surviving violence has also helped me reach one of the most profoundly difficult conclusions that I have ever had to make. Specifically, I have decided that perceiving ourselves as having ultimate control over our destinies is vain self-delusion. Coming to accept the fact that I actually have very little control over most aspects of my life has been a bitter pill for me to swallow. Because I have always perceived myself to be the ultimate self-determinate individualist, admitting I was wrong has been terribly difficult. But I concede now that I never had the degree of control over my life that I wanted to believe.

Violence is a perfect example of one event in life that exists totally beyond our control.

If we look closely, we can see many other circumstances that show that we cannot unilaterally direct our lives. Global politics, international economics, even the weather and traffic, are classic examples of those things over which we have little or no control. Yet they have the potential to completely alter our lives, or end them in an instant. To admit our true impotence in this respect may be a humbling experience, but I believe it represents the only way we can regain a realistic perspective of this world and thus allow ourselves to better live within the constraints of its realities.

Becoming a statistic of violence has also clearly shown me that we victims have inherited certain obligations with our tragedy.

First, we have an obligation to ourselves and those we care most about to overcome the emotional destruction we have experienced. Many times during my recovery process, the only motivator I could find for not giving in to despair was my determination not to allow my mother's killer to ruin my life and the lives of my family as a result.

He defeated me once when he murdered my mother and escaped justice, and I remain powerless to change this outcome, regardless of how much it infuriates me. I refuse, however, to allow him to control the remainder of my life by surrendering to my anger and resentment over this fact. Applying the adage "He who controls my thoughts, controls my life" is a fundamental requirement for everyone who must overcome the consequences of violence.

I hope that other survivors will consider my suggestion that we also have an obligation to others who become the victims of violence. That is, only those who have survived the crucible of violence can truly understand and empathize with the needs of its victims. Therefore, I feel that we should consider sharing whatever we may have to offer with those who need our support. I believe that violence represents one of those tragedies in life that bring with it responsibilities that only a select few can fulfill.

Our assistance may take many forms. Certainly, involvement in survivor support groups can be a tremendously important resource for those in need of help. Other survivors I know have become advocates for the cause of victims' rights. Truth in sentencing laws, victims' rights statutes, and victims' advocate services within law enforcement all represent gains obtained because of these activists. Others may establish their niche through poetry or writing. Many people, including myself, have found inspiration in the words of victims who share burdens similar to their own.

My long battle for survival has also forced me to seriously examine a critical point of faith that at one time jeopardized the very nature of my relationship with God. I refer to those inexpressibly desperate days when I pleaded with God to demonstrate His presence in my life, seemingly to no avail. While even now I doubt that I will ever fully understand this enigma, I do believe that I understand the nature of faith better because of what I have experienced.

Questions regarding God's role in this world and His involvement in our lives always seem to reflect how much faith we have in His ability to consistently, without exception, do what is right. If we believe that God is literally incapable of doing anything but that which is right, good, and just, then we must assume that He is always working for our welfare as believers. This applies in even the most incomprehensible conditions.

Examining my own circumstances in retrospect, the fact that I did not feel His presence at times does not mean that He was not with me. In fact, I believe that He is unceasingly loving and supportive of me, so I must assume that He was there with me all along. My emotions, though, led me to believe otherwise. Given the tremendous power of those emotions I was experiencing—hatred, resentment, bitterness, frustration, despair and depression—it becomes somewhat easier now to recognize that these overwhelming influences probably distorted my perspective of everything in my life, particularly God's presence.

I cannot leave the topic of God's involvement in this world without taking one last look at the role that our prayers to Him play in all of this. As one who lives daily with a sense of confusion surrounding the lack of answers I have so often sought in prayer, I am forcing myself to recognize that we simply cannot determine our prayers to be failures based upon how we interpret the answers.

We do not possess the unlimited perspective that only God has to make such determinations for ourselves. Faith again tells me that God is perfect, and as such, by the very nature of His perfection, He cannot forsake our prayers. I have to believe that He is in the process of providing me some response to my questions, although I may never see it in this lifetime.

Nevertheless, I have had to dramatically reassess what I am willing to submit to God in the form of prayer. The focus of my prayer requests now centers much more upon my desire for Him to influence my life rather than alter those circumstances affecting my life. Admittedly, old habits die hard, and I often find myself wanting to request His intervention in a particular circumstance. Still, the realistic part of my nature seriously questions the legitimacy of expecting God to intervene in the course of events in this universe solely for my benefit. For this reason, I am skeptical of the appropriateness of requesting circumstantial specifics from God.

Consider the familiar example of travel. I know many people, including good friends for whom I have much respect, who are in the habit of requesting God's intercession for the sake of those they care about, when traveling. Perhaps it's my skeptical victim/police nature, but I cannot realistically accept that God will prevent the often-deadly actions of the thousands of drunken, belligerent, oblivious, or texting drivers inundating our streets and highways today. While I must believe that in some rare and exceptional cases He does somehow miraculously save people from such tragedies, statistics bear out the fact that He does not do so in the 40,000 traffic fatalities that occur every year in this country.

Therefore, instead of praying for His intercession in such a situation, my approach to prayer today focuses on asking Him to help me (or whomever I may be concerned for) use good driving judgment, display patience, be critically observant of conditions, and always be on guard for danger. While this may not afford me as much peace of mind as the other alternative, I am convinced that it is a much more realistic practice of faith and prayer.

Essentially, I have concluded that in my humanity, I am entitled to sometimes feel confused, abandoned, and even angry at God because I do not perceive my prayers to have accomplished the desired result. Nevertheless, I don't have the right to let this become a lasting barrier to my relationship with the Lord of my life. At some point, whether I like it or not, I have to relinquish my battle for control and let God be God, both in how He manages this world and how He chooses to honor my requests of prayer.

Perhaps the single most significant insight I have gained as a victim is the realization that I am involved in an emotional recovery process that will actually be ongoing for the remainder of my life. Since I will carry the scars of violence with me until I die, I must accept that complete recovery from what I have experienced will always be a continuing effort, a goal always before me but never quite achieved.

As such, I have concluded that my recovery from violence can only be achieved one step at a time, much like the alcoholic achieves sobriety one day at a time. Trying to carry this emotional cross, to escape its grasp of hopelessness and despair, to rebuild my life cannot be done in a single effort. Just like achieving sanctification in a Christian context is a never-ending process, so is recovering from emotional carnage of the magnitude experienced by those of us surviving violence.

I cannot possibly expect to accomplish this transformation overnight. I have found that accepting this fact releases me from a tremendous emotional burden, and I hope this realization will provide comfort to other survivors.

We cannot be expected to "get on with our lives" just as if nothing ever happened. We should not feel guilty because we can't "heal old wounds" or "keep our chins up" as we are expected to "get over" what we have experienced. A major part of our core selves died in that violence, and it is impossible for us not to be different people than we once were. We don't owe anyone apologies for what has happened to us, nor do we have to make excuses for the changes in our personalities that have been the result.

We must, however, recognize that we do stand at a fork in the road leading to our ultimate destination. Despite all we have endured, we still have a choice as to how we will incorporate into our future the horrible realities we have experienced.

On one hand, we can choose to embrace our bitterness, our resentment, our hatred of all that has victimized us. We can conclude that the world is filled with hateful and violent people and emotionally isolate ourselves from everyone else as a result. In short, we can give up on the world, give in to our despair, and allow our future to be controlled by the past.

There is another option available to us, however. This is the one I believe Victor Frankl was referring to when he spoke of choosing the right response to the worst of circumstances. To follow this path means making the commitment to rise above the devastation that has been inflicted upon us. And while it represents the greatest commitment and the most work, I believe it offers us the only road back to lasting emotional and spiritual health.

Taking this road means that we are willing to commit our energies to serving the best elements of this world, not the worst. It means relying upon the best within our nature, not the scarred and battered worst within us. It requires accepting that while there exist

THE SHADOW OF EVIL

in this world forces of unspeakable evil and vileness, we have chosen to live our lives on a higher plane. It dictates that we will strive for the good of ourselves and those around us. Choosing this option also means recognizing that we are committing to a lifelong process that we can never achieve solely through our own efforts.

Here again I draw a parallel from the world of all 12-step people. Just as alcoholics must learn to admit that their recovery is a lifelong, one-day-at-a-time effort, they also come to accept that the magnitude of the task is too large for them to accomplish by themselves.

That is why they ultimately have to place their faith in God if they ever hope to achieve sobriety. Therefore, I believe that we who constitute the world of survivors must sooner or later recognize that if we ever hope to achieve our own goal of emotional recovery, we can only accomplish this through the strength of God Himself.

I believe it is impossible for any of us to adequately reconstruct our lives, dramatically redefine who we are and what we believe, completely overcome our emotional trauma, successfully adopt a positive perspective of the world, and ultimately overcome our hatred of those who sought to destroy us, without an unequivocal reliance on the power of God.

As much as this admission of weakness may run contrary to our self-sufficient, independent human nature, my own experience tells me I have no choice. At every critical juncture in the past, I have always found myself in need of the Lord's assistance. Therefore, as I approach my most difficult task ever, I am forced to accept that only by trusting completely in God can this goal ever become reality for me.

This is because no matter how strong my desire is to rebuild my life, no matter what commitment I make to regain my emotional well-being, no matter how determined I am to transcend the past, I realize that the forces against my success are too overwhelming. My lifelong pessimistic perspective of the world cannot be abandoned that easily. The rage I feel toward the one responsible for Mother's murder still seethes within me. The bitterness from failing to bring closure to her case cuts like a razor into the very fiber of my nature. My resentment at God's long-suffering patience in bringing justice upon even the most vile and wicked among us continues to frustrate me. This is the magnitude of the obstacles I will have to overcome to achieve my recovery.

In the process, many questions will have to be answered.

Will I ever be able to get beyond my mistrust of people because of what one wicked human being did to my mother? Is my faith in God strong enough to put aside my anger and resentment resulting from her murder? Can I summon the powers of tenacity passed on to me by my dad in order to successfully rebuild my life? Is my dedication to family strong enough to keep my commitment to not relinquish my life to bitterness, resentment, and cynicism? Can I overcome the terrible days of loneliness and depression that make the battle for survival sometimes seem hopeless?

To each of these questions I can only answer that I honestly don't know. Time alone will tell. Still, I maintain a hope that eventually I will be able to answer these positively.

Finally, I wish I could conclude by stating that Mother's murder has resulted in some profoundly positive insights about life that would have been unattainable under ordinary circumstances. While I have searched desperately for something—anything—that would confirm this, I am afraid I still come away empty-handed.

As much as I would like to attribute some meaning to her death, I still see it as the ultimate futility—the waste of a wonderful life for no conceivable reason. A kind, selfless, loving lady died alone that night at the hands of the vilest perversion of mankind. And lost with her was a tremendous source of love and enrichment to the lives of all who knew her and loved her.

Our society as a whole was also degraded by her death, just as it is each time a human being is victimized by violence. We all lose some of our optimism in the forces of good, our trust in the virtue of our fellowman, our hopes for a better tomorrow, our faith in God's justice, our sense of personal well-being, and our idealism toward life. These were among the subtle casualties of violence that were inflicted upon all of us the night my mother died. In this sense, her death demeaned the life of every other person who shares this world with me.

Perhaps my unspoken mission from now on will be to ensure that something positive results from her murder. Since I can see nothing constructive yet, I may have to use my own willpower and determination to ensure that her death ultimately attains some value. I owe that much to my mother. I believe she would expect me to make the most of even this intolerable situation.

The legacy she left me was to make something good from the very worst, to not be dragged down and defeated by all the negative influences surrounding me. Even now, on the other side of eternity, I can almost hear her telling me, "Hon, you've got to keep searching for something positive, some good to come out of this. You can't let this destroy you."

I believe my dad is also there with her, just as he always was with me on the sidelines at those football games, telling me not to quit making the extra effort to make that next tackle. I can picture him in my mind saying, "Son, remember, giving up is not an option in this family. We have never tolerated quitters, and you know it. You'll find a way to get beyond this. Remember your heritage. You can't quit."

So it is my hope—for the sake of their memories—that I will eventually come to see something beneficial ensue from Mother's death. Maybe if I can learn to truly appreciate the present, to take time out for those precious moments that will never again be, then her death will not have been in vain. Perhaps if I can ever learn to live my life one day at a time, not worrying about the future or victimizing myself with the past, then her death will assume some meaning. If I can be successful at turning over every aspect of my life to God as I make this long journey toward recovery, then perhaps she will smile, content with the knowledge that her death did accomplish something worthwhile after all.

Maybe then I will eventually come to see that she did not die in vain, but instead, through her death, offered us all the opportunity to seriously examine the manner in which we approach this sojourn called life. Maybe... just maybe.

AFTERWORD

The call that I had waited fourteen years for came in around 7:00 p.m. on Friday, February 25, 2005. Work obligations had brought me to Memphis little more than a year before, and I was settling into a weekly routine of playing pool on Friday nights whenever possible. I was with a couple of friends from work and was on a bit of a hot streak when my phone rang. Not really wanting to interrupt my game, I almost didn't pick up, but events earlier in day told me that I probably should. The voice on the other end was that of Sam Houston, onetime lead investigator on Mother's case with the Sedgwick County Sheriff's Office. He said, "Jeff, we got him. We caught the guy who killed your mom." He went on to tell me the man was named Dennis Rader. He was fifty-nine years old, and he had confessed to murdering my mother. I was stunned and overwhelmed at once. We talked on for a few more minutes and left it that he would call me when he knew more.

Obviously that call put an end to pool night, and I quickly got into my car and headed back to my apartment, my head swirling with what this news meant. My overriding thought was, they got him! After all these years of tormenting questions and endless uncertainty, my prayers had been answered! My mind raced on. *Who is this Rader? How did they catch him? Had he killed anyone else?*

So many questions, but still too early for answers.

I whiled away the rest of that evening hoping to hear more, but at that point, there was not much else being released by the news media, only that Rader was in the custody of the Wichita Police Department and more information would be forthcoming when available. Eventually, once all the adrenaline had worn off, I realized

I was out of gas, so I went to bed, hoping tomorrow would provide me more information.

That next morning, Saturday, initiated a blitz of activity that wouldn't completely wind down until Rader's eventual conviction and incarceration six months later. My fiancée called me early that morning to notify me that the Wichita Police Department would soon be holding a news conference of great importance. I tuned in just in time to hear then Police Chief Norm Williams announce proudly, "The bottom line: BTK is arrested!" He went on to say that the subject, Dennis Rader, a resident of Park City, Kansas, had been arrested yesterday afternoon by Wichita Police detectives Kelly Otis and Kenny Landwehr.

The pieces were beginning to fall into place; it was starting to make sense now. I had believed all along that my mother was the victim of a serial killer, and I had always been outspoken about it. And I had known about the BTK ever since he murdered the Otero family shortly after I had graduated Wichita State. However, because of the length of time between his last known victim, Maurine Hedge, in 1986, and my mother's murder in 1991, I had failed to connect the dots, as had law enforcement.

Known to the community by the name BTK, which he had so proudly given himself through the media, Rader had represented true horror: bind, torture, and kill were his MO, ensuring a slow and painful death for each of his victims. Here he was, now in custody, the notorious BTK serial killer who had previously murdered nine innocent people, including two children, in a spree of terror stretching from 1974 to 1991. He and the heretofore phantom that killed my mother were now one!

I could hardly process it all. But even if I could have reasoned my way through everything at that point, I had no time. My phone immediately began ringing and continued incessantly throughout the entire day. Media outlet after media outlet was calling me, wanting to know my reaction to the arrest. Had I suspected the BTK in Mom's case? Had I ever heard the name *Dennis Rader*? How did I suppose he came across my mother? Far too many questions for which I didn't have answers.

***

The next several months rolled by fairly quickly as Rader's case moved through the justice system. His preliminary hearing (an appearance before a judge in which a plea of guilty or not guilty is entered) was set for the month of June. At his prelim, Rader pled guilty, thus eliminating the time and expense of a trial. Instead, there would be a sentencing hearing on August 17, 2005, at which time all relevant facts would be presented to a judge, who would then pronounce sentence on Rader.

Throughout all this time, I was contacted by countless media outlets requesting interviews, most of which I was happy to provide. I think it was cathartic to have a forum through which I could express my feelings, and the media seemed to enjoy my hard-hitting and politically incorrect comments about Rader and his trail of destruction. I approached every interview as if Rader himself was watching, and I assumed at times he actually would be, given the county jail had television for the inmates. I wanted this to be personal between me and Rader, and for good reason.

I had received two letters after my mother's murder, one the summer of 1991, then another right after this book's first edition was released in 1996 (see addendum 2). Once the case was closed, Wichita Police detectives Otis and Landwehr had been able to confirm my suspicions that both letters were written by Rader. We could see that there was a mix of fact and fantasy in each, but both were pointedly intended to taunt me. He had relished the fact that he was one up on me and wanted me to know it. For that reason, my many scathing and caustic comments in these interviews were targeted directly at him. He had wanted it to be personal between the two of us, and so I made sure it was.

The first day of Rader's sentencing hearing will stay with me forever. I woke up that morning, Wednesday, August 17, thinking, at last, after I had long since given up on the thought of ever seeing him face justice in this world, here it was, time for him to pay, and I couldn't wait to witness it. Not only were my own family members in attendance in the courtroom—Amy, my daughter; Jason, my son; Nan, their mother; and Monie, my fiancée—but members of the families representing his other nine victims would be there as well. Each family member would have the opportunity to sit through all the proceedings, and at the end, we would all be able to deliver our own victim impact statements describing the dreadful impact his actions had had upon our lives.

As I sat in the courtroom listening to grisly police testimony and looking at photos of my mother's crime scene (some of which I refused to look at), a thought came to me. For years I had begged God for answers, at times demanding that he provide me with each and every detail surrounding her murder. How ironic it was, then, that I was getting my answers, no matter how painful these were turning out to be. He had honored my prayers by answering all but the elusive *why*, and I doubt that even Rader himself could satisfactorily answer that one. In return, I was left with the emotional scars of seeing and hearing all the terror my mother endured in her last moments on earth. A costly trade-off, I will admit.

Once all testimony had concluded, it was time for the victims' families to have their say. Each of us was afforded the opportunity to read our impact statements, prepared in advance (see addendum 1). One by one, often while choking back sobs and wiping away tears, each person tried to describe the hell they had lived through in the wake of Rader's sadistic and murderous acts. At one point, I asked myself, *How much pain and anguish can one person unleash on this world?* There I sat, listening to one tearful litany after another detailing the irreparable damage that one narcissistic, sociopathic misanthrope had caused, and it was almost impossible to comprehend the magnitude of heartache in that courtroom that day.

On the last day, Friday, August 19, Judge Greg Waller sentenced Rader to ten life sentences, 175 years specifically—the maximum allowed by Kansas law, thus ensuring that he would never leave prison alive. I think this fact met with the approval of most family members, mine included. Still, the unspoken thought we all shared was that nothing could ever bring our loved ones back. That realization left me with a sense of emptiness and futility. While I relished the thought of Rader languishing away in an eight–by-ten cell twenty-three hours a day for the rest of his wretched existence, I knew full well the only thing that could ever bring me happiness was to have my mother back, and that was never to be. I suspected that many of the other family members felt much as I did, all of us concluding that this entire proceeding had been a hollow victory at best.

Once the hearing was over and Rader began serving his sentence, people would inevitably ask me if all this had finally allowed me to find closure in my mother's murder. My simple answer was, no, it hadn't. By that I mean, for me, closure would be going back to the instant before she died, and somehow redirecting the course of events so as to allow her to remain in my life, which is, of course, impossible. Therefore, achieving closure, to my way of thinking, is impossible.

We often discuss, in the context of violent loss, the need for victims and survivors to achieve closure. And on the surface, who could argue with that? However, I believe the issue at play runs deeper. Of course we all would like to say we've reached closure, and to some degree perhaps we do. But I believe we are really talking more about reconciliation and resolution than we are about closure per se.

By that I believe that we survivors can eventually reconcile our conflicting mix of emotions resulting from our loss in a way that allows us to maintain an emotionally healthy perspective of life. We can't change all that has occurred, but we can reconcile with that loss by integrating it into the whole of who we are. We can find some degree of resolution once some of our questions have been answered and the guilty have been brought to justice. Nonetheless, my interpretation of true closure means that all is well and we will live happily ever after, just as we had prior to our tragedy, and everyone knows this just isn't so. Those recovering from violent loss know their lives will never be the same, and the best we can do is accept that reality and move forward in our lives with that perspective.

Of all the lessons I've learned along this long road to recovery, probably the most challenging, and the one I continue to wrestle with most, is the realization that God still allows evil free reign in this world at the expense of us all. For whatever reason, He continues to permit evil to overshadow good, the wicked to slay the innocent, the perverse to overwhelm the righteous, year after year, seemingly without end. We hear daily of an endless parade of atrocities playing out everywhere in the world: depraved ISIS fanatics crucify young children and behead Christians; an illegal alien deported from this county multiple times shoots and kills a young lady at San Francisco's Fisherman's Wharf for no apparent reason; two radical Islamic terrorists detonate a bomb at the Boston marathon, killing and maiming innocents; a hate-filled extremist ambushes and murders five police officers in Dallas. Who can blame any of us for asking, "How long, how long, Lord, must this go on?"

On a cognitive level, I think I understand why evil is allowed to persist. God gave mankind the gift of free will from the outset in His Eden. But man's evil has turned that gift of free will into the curse of free will, which has served as our undoing ever since. I recognize that for God to have done anything else would have made us His robots, with Him controlling our every move, and that wouldn't work for either Him or us. His desire is that we freely love Him and seek a personal relationship with Him. That is something that He can't force upon us; it has to be initiated by us, and only through the free will He gave us can we make that choice.

It is the abuse of our free will and the immeasurable pain it causes in this world that we find so hard to accept. In my case, God gave a sadistic murderer named Dennis Rader his own free will, and Rader perverted it in order to justify his torturing and slowly killing ten innocent people. Moreover, his horrific acts left in its wake untold suffering for the victims' friends and families left behind, ensuring that his legacy of evil endures still.

So part of my learning in the wake of my mother's murder tells me that I must accept the fact that the evil of this world will continue to wreak havoc and destruction on the innocent and wicked alike, until God decides to intervene with His Second Coming. Until then, I feel our challenge is to walk that fine line between reconciling the reality that evil will continue to cause pain and suffering in this world, while not losing our faith in the goodness of God and the divine glory of His plan for our lives.

I look one last time to the book of Job for some direction as I ponder the question of why God allows bad things to happen to good people. Job never did get any explanation from God as to why he had to suffer so much heartache and tragedy. However, what God did do in return was wholly restore Job's life, affording him a new family and the renewal of all his wealth, even more than what he had had originally. What this tells me is that while God may not always provide us with answers to our most vexing questions, He does always have our best interests in mind. While it is often not apparent to me, my faith tells me that God is working for good in my life through all things, even the times when I am railing at Him the loudest in disagreement!

Finally, I believe one critical last topic deserves attention. That is, what role our faith in God plays in all of this. Job endured immeasurable tragedy before finally being renewed and restored—a goal most of us survivors hope to see come to pass in our own lives. However, I strongly believe that the key to Job being able to move from despair to hope was his remaining faithful to God. Throughout his travails, Job could have easily chosen to abandon his faith at any number of junctures. But he held firm to his faith in spite of overwhelming adversity and doubt. And I believe this to be the crux of the issue and the key to our being able to get beyond our own heartache, not giving up our faith in Him.

God may not have restored Job's life to fullness if Job had not kept his faith and instead chosen to follow his wife's advice to "curse God and die" (Job 2:9). Instead, his words were incredibly simple but set "the bar of faith" very high. He responded to his wife's goading by replying he had come into the world with nothing and he would leave this world with nothing, noting that God gives and God takes away. Then he blessed the Lord's name. What an incredible example of unwavering faith!

How many of us, upon losing our entire family, all our worldly possessions, even our health, our lives in utter ruin and despair, could model Job's example of unquestioning faith and still remain true to God? I must confess, I for one would likely not come close to being able to uphold this tremendous example of selfless faith.

And I suppose that represents the last challenge in my continued sojourn toward recovery. Can I finally accept the reality that God does not run the world according to my expectations, but instead according to his perfect plan? Is my faith strong enough to believe that He does answer my prayers, even when I can't see the immediate result? Can I maintain my faith that God is working for good in my life always, even in the times when I feel nothing but doubt, uncertainty, confusion, and fear? Can I reconcile within my faith the fact that the shadow of evil will continue to darken and degrade all our lives until God finally decides enough is enough and rights the scales of justice in this world? I hope so.

Are these the last of the questions I'll have as I continue my journey of recovery? I seriously doubt it. However, I am prepared to address those concerns *if* and *when* the time comes. I'm confident I can do so by reflecting upon all I have overcome to get to this point, by understanding how those circumstances have influenced who I am today, and by trusting God to provide me with whatever I need to live out His will for my life.

If you love me, do not weep. If you only knew the gift of God and what heaven is! If only you could hear the angels' song from where you are and see me among them! If you could only see before your eyes the eternal fields with their horizons, and the new paths in which I walk! If only you could contemplate for one moment the beauty I see. Beauty before which others fail and fade!

Why do you who saw me and loved me in the land of shadows, why do you think you will not see me and love me again in the land of unchanging realities?

Believe me, when death breaks your chains, as it has broken mine, when, on the day chosen by God, your soul reaches heaven where I have preceded you, then you will see her who loved and still loves you. You will find her heart the same, her tenderness even purer than before.

God forbid that on entering a happier life, I should become less loving, unfaithful to the memories and real joys of my other life. You will see me again, transfigured in ecstasy and happiness, no longer waiting for death, but ever hand in hand with you, walking in the new paths of light and life, slaking my thirst to the full at the feet of God from a fount of which one never tires, and which you will come to share with me.

Wipe away your tears, and if you love me truly, weep no more.

—Words of Saint Monica to Saint Augustine

ADDENDUM 1

Author's note: I am including this addendum in order to share with you the only interaction I ever had with the man who took my mother's life. I am including this because it is part of the official court transcript, but also because it is indicative of where I was emotionally on that day in 2005. Upon hearing these words at the time, some found them to be harsh and off-putting. Many others, particularly those representing the survivors of homicide victims, felt that my message expressed exactly what they too felt. My intent is that you, the reader, will review it and decide for yourself.

Jeffrey M. Davis's Victim Impact Statement, delivered August 19, 2005, before the Honorable Judge Greg Waller and directed to Dennis Rader

***

May it please the court to allow me to express my thoughts and feelings to all the victim survivors here among us today in the hope that we can leave this troubled courtroom with some sense of internal peace and legal resolution.

For the last 5,326 days I have wondered what it would be like to confront the walking cesspool that took my mother's precious life. Throughout that time I always envisioned this day as being one for avenging the past. I could think of nothing but savoring the bittersweet taste of revenge as justice is served upon this sewage here before us today. Now that it has arrived, surprisingly, I realize that this day is not about avenging crimes past.

Sitting here before us is a depraved predator, a rabid animal that has murdered innocent people, poisoned countless lives, and terrorized this community for 30 years, while relishing every minute of it. As such, there can be no justice harsh enough or revenge bitter enough (in this world at least) to cause the pain and suffering which a social malignancy like this has coming. Therefore, I have determined that for the sake of our innocent victims and their loving families and friends with us here today, for me this will be a day of celebration, not retribution.

If my focus were hatred, I would stare you down and call you the devil's ilk, which defiles this court at the very sight of its cancerous presence.

If I embraced bitterness, I would remind you that you are nothing but a despicable, child-molesting, woman-hating, impotent little pervert masquerading as a human being.

If I were the animal that you are, I would say that I relish the thought of you being treated to the same despicable brutality, terror, and agony at the hands of your soon-to-be fellow inmates, that you relished inflicting on your defenseless victims.

If I were spiteful, I would remind you that it is only fitting that a twisted, narcissistic psychopath, obsessed with public attention, will soon have his world reduced to an isolated, solitary existence, doomed to languish away the rest of your miserable life, alone, in an 80 sq. ft. cell.

If I had your animal soul, I would delight in the fact that your congregation has turned its back on you, that your friends have deserted you, that your wife has divorced you, that your own children have disowned you, and then I would remind you that you will never have any warm, loving human contact again for the remainder of your twisted existence.

If I were cynical, I would remind this court that you would return to your murderous ways in a heartbeat if given the opportunity, so for the safety of society, you must remain caged forever like any other viscous, predatory animal.

If I were to sink to your level, I would say that this world would have been much better off had your demon soul been aborted before you were unleashed on this world, sparing ten innocent lives and avoiding untold heartache for this community.

If I were vindictive, I would wish you many long, emotionally tortured years in your cage, haunted every night by your victim's hopeless pleas for mercy as you played God and pronounced their death sentences upon them.

If I had your sadistic nature, I would delight in the pain you feel in now realizing that your own arrogance and ego got you caught, that if you had just kept your big mouth shut, you would still be a free man today.

If I wanted revenge, I would pray that you develop a lingering, agonizing illness, from which you suffer for many, many years before you ultimately choke to death one lonely night on your own vomit.

If I were judgmental, I would call you the most despicable form of hypocrite for profaning Christianity by daring to associate yourself with my faith and for blaspheming God's house with your demonic actions.

If I were unforgiving, I would tell you that I will accept any shameful, meaningless attempts on your part to feign remorse by responding that I will grant you forgiveness the same day that hell freezes over, although I know my mother in her Christian grace has long since forgiven you.

But I won't hurl these invectives at you, or rain these curses down upon you, because you're not smart enough to understand most of the words I'd use anyway. And even if you could understand the depths of my hatred for you, I still refuse to waste any breath on you because that would once again allow you the satisfaction of being in the limelight, and that attention I refuse to allow you. Today, the focus finally moves out from under your depraved shadow of hell's darkness, into the light of your victims and their families. Speaking for my mother, with us in spirit, for my own family, and I hope for the entire family of survivors here today, we dedicate this day to the memories of those who cannot be with us. Today we also celebrate with this community the relief in knowing that we will never again be victimized by a monster's demented fantasies.

Today, we will each silently remember a father, a brother, a wife, a mother, a sister, a daughter, a grandmother—all those who we loved so deeply and miss so dearly still. Today, we will quietly reminisce on all they meant to us, we will smile at the silly things they did that made us laugh, and we will renew our pride in who they were. Today, we will thank them for shaping our lives, for being there when we needed them, for setting the example of what we should be, for making us who we are, and for allowing us to be their living legacies.

From this point on, we declare our independence from the tyranny of your actions. While you begin your slow and painful descent into hell, we will choose to rise above our pain. While you sink into an emotional abyss of hopelessness and despair, we will channel our grief into positive endeavors, those life activities that would please the ones we have lost. While you agonize over the reality that your last victims were ironically your own family, we will embrace the new family we now have, with whom we will always share a common bond forged from the pain of adversity and loss. While your body wastes away in prison, we will renew our selves by incorporating into our lives those character traits modeled by our loved ones: humility, compassion, honor, integrity, kindness, selflessness, and love—traits that your twisted, cancerous mind cannot comprehend, I realize. While your wretched soul awaits pronouncement of the one true justice, your damnation to hell for eternity, we will thank God for every day He gives us, realizing as only we can, just how precious life really is.

Finally, we want you to know that we, who could so easily have drowned in your cesspool of madness, will not give you that satisfaction. Your despicable actions will not defeat us. Our very lives will be testimony that good can prevail over even the most hideous form of evil and perversion. Just as your days are now over, ours are just beginning. At long, long last, we can all smile and say to you, we win, you lose!

Thank you, Your Honor.

ADDENDUM 2

Author's note: I include these letters within this book, not to give the impression of pandering to cheap sensationalism, but to provide the reader with some unique and revealing insights into the mind of a serial murderer.

Rader sent these to me for the purpose of taunting me, as evidenced in several of the statements he makes. He mixes some fact with a lot of fantasy, but you will also note a number of typographical and spelling errors attesting to his marginal IQ. These typos, misspellings, and specific typeset were what allowed WPD detectives to confirm that these collectively matched other letters they had in their possession known to be from him.

Herein are two letters from Dennis Rader to myself, the author. One arrived in June 1991, about six months after my mother's death; the other arrived in the spring of 1996, shortly after the first edition of this book was published. Both were later determined by Wichita Police Detectives to have been written by Dennis Rader

Dear Sir:

First, a woman went to the police with serious complaints about a destructive religious cult and they did not even take a report. They did not so much as make an effort to solve and/or punish the wrongdoer. Even after about 2 million dollars worth of damage, they yawned in her face.

Second, we believe that the man who killed Delores Davis probably killed Vickie Lynn Wegerle in Sept. 1986.

Third, he probably wants to go back to his original state (not of Original Sin as before baptism) but of his original state of being pure, holy and well thought of. And he can't because of a sexual addiction.

God keep you in His living care.

May 24, 1996

Wichita, Ks.

Dear Mr. Davis:

First of all, thanks so much for writing your book,
The Shadow of Evil: Where is God In a Violent World?
I am so grateful that you expressed many of the same emotions
that I've experienced when confronted with evil and violence.
Even though I've never had a loved one killed by violence, except
for the war, we did have a son who sustained two brutal assaults
after he was targeted by a gang. Also, I suffered emotional and
spiritual devastation when I was the victim of a cult.

Just so you'll know where I'm coming from, I'm 60+ years-
old, am white of ethnic origin, have an average education, and
have lived in Northern Sedgwick County for 30+ (thirty) years
now. That's a long, long time.

By NOrthern Sedgwick I mean it in the broader sense--to
include parts of West Wichita. I'm not just talking about past
the city limits.

Personally, I believe that the same man did kill Marine
Hedge, Vicki Wegerle and your mother. There seems to be
similarities among all of these cases. And, of course, differences,
too.

163

-2-

For example, Marine Hedge allegedly had knotted panyhose found near her body. And Vicki was allegedly strangled, and the killer moved her car. I really did not know until I read your book that the killer might have moved your mother's body in her own vehicle. I really can't believe that anyone would do that, because he would have had to leave his own car somewhere nearby. That's truly risky, especially after breaking glass.

Also, you said that you didn't know what the mask represented. Neither do I. However, some people believe that he didn't have it that night, but he may have come back the following week and placed it there. Of course, he was the only one who knew where her body was. I'm not even sure what that kind of mask is. But, we have created a fictional story to explain what the stacking of the shoes into a pyramid-like figure might mean, if that is what actually happened. We'll call the serial killer, The Phantom of Northern Sedwick County. Here is what he might say, if you could actually talk with him:

> To me, the pyramid represents power--the kind that goes on forever. I can represent Jesus for the Devil. We all can. However, in my case, I go from one extreme to the other; but, I only switch to the Devil in the presence of my carefully selected victims.
>
> Actually, the only reason I chose your mother was that she resembled and did talk like my lost love, Lilly, I call her Lil. As you know, after your mother's death, one man said that your mother was very, nice-looking, and had a gentle, cultured way of talking to people. So did my Lil.

-3-

After ten years of dating Lil, and driving many,
many miles to see her, she actually had the
nerve to tell me that she was moving across country
with her husband. They lived in a big, beautiful
home just off of <u>W. 21st</u>, west of Meridian, near
the bridge. I.....I just couldn't bear the pain
nor the humiliation. Through the years, I have
made a big Fool out of myself and others all for
her. Now she was abandoning me like my mother did
so many years before.

WICHITA

Today, when I think of Lil abandoning me, I always
replace that image with the one of your mother lying
out in that remote area, west of Meridian, under-
neath the bridge. By doing this, I've replaced
pain with power, albeit temporarily.

Living with self-delusions,

The Phantom of Northern Sedgwick County

Even though this sounds crazy, I'm sure that he probably

blends in with a crowd, He might even be charming, many of the

serial killers are known to be. And even if he didn't kill those

other two women, you know that he's killed before, because one

just doesn't start off with barging through a glass door. I'm

sure your mother was terrified.

With the other two, Vicki Wegerle and Marine Hedge, Vicki

probably opened the door to someone she knew from her

volunteer work. And Marine probably went for a ride with

someone she had met at the hospital.

Finally, we will pray that you get some answers someday.

But even if you don't, you have written a good book, and will

help many people with it. My heart pounded during that part

where you went back on the anniversary of your mother's death,

to sit and wait for the killer. It's too bad that "Unsolved

Mysteries" didn't accept this story. It would have been an

interesting one, and would have adapted well to the screen.

Bless you.   A Taxpayer (N. Sedgwick County)

ACKNOWLEDGMENTS

When I first set out to write edition 1 of this book all those years ago, I had no idea it would take the help and collaboration of so many friends and family members to make it a reality. Now that edition 2 is finally complete, I would like to thank again all those who were instrumental in allowing me to complete this project, then and now.

I owe a great deal of thanks to all who were involved in the tedious editing process. Specifically, this includes Carol Kaloger, Duane Patrick, Larry and Joy Jeffries, Judy Turner, and Bill Wise. My edition 1 editor, Darlene Hoffa deserves special recognition for being a master at knowing how to transform a rough manuscript into finished copy. I really appreciate the time and effort you put in on this project.

Those who offered comments from a legal perspective include Tom Turner, John Spence III, Lawson Lamar, Jim Wardell, and Eva Doppelt. Thank you for sharing your expertise.

Russ Phillips provided comments from a mental health perspective, which helped me considerably.

To my law enforcement associates, I am also indebted. Specifically, (former) Major Jim Elvins of the Sedgwick County Sheriff's Office, Officer David Manning of the Fort Worth Police Department, and Ellen Hanson, (former) chief of police, Lenexa Police Department, were very helpful in providing their input.

All of you who represent victim advocate groups were instrumental to the success of this project. I could not have completed this book without the help of Nancy Ruhe-Munch, Corinne Radke, Jean and Joe Teneriello, Steve Zellers, and Carol and Jim Kaloger from Parents of Murdered Children. Greta Snitkin, with Bereaved Survivors of Homicide, also contributed countless hours responding to my requests for assistance. I owe a special thanks to Sharon English, Office for Victims of Crime, for sharing with me her wealth of knowledge regarding victims' issues.

I am particularly indebted to my friends Coni Patrick and James Caldwell for their technical assistance with edition 1. I truly appreciate the time you each devoted to the completion of the cover design and interior layout.

My old friend and former pastor, Ralph Barclay, contributed a great deal by providing me his thoughts from a ministerial perspective. I wish to express my thanks to Father Peter Gilguist and Burt Wilkins, who shared their Christian views with me on this subject.

Since it is impossible to personally recognize every individual friend and family member who contributed to this project, please accept my heartfelt thanks at this point, anyone whom I may have inadvertently failed to recognize.

I want to extend my warmest thanks to my sister Laurel; my two wonderful, now-grown children, Amy and Jason; and their mother, Nan Davis, who were so patient with me during one of the darkest periods of our lives as I worked to coax edition 1 to life. Without all their patience and support, this book would never have happened.

I especially want to recognize those involved in making edition 2 a reality, my wife, Monie, and my publishing team at Christian Faith Publishing. Monie I thank for her patience and persistence in helping me organize and proof the book through each stage of development and for forgiving my exasperation whenever she found another mistake I did not want to acknowledge. My "publishing coach", Leslie Hargenrater was a saint in fielding all my myriad questions and patiently explaining the process whenever I needed assistance. Her team in editing, layout, and graphic arts provided me much needed and very helpful direction throughout the publication process. You guys are great!

And lastly, I can't leave out my two work associates, Bill Gray and Andrew Norton, who were the catalysts most recently in planting the seed in my mind to move forward with edition 2. After listening to all my excuses for not doing it, they put it to me simply: "Try it and see what happens. What do you have to lose?" Thanks so much for not taking "no" for my answer and thus ensuring that edition 2 became reality!

NOTES

PREFACE
1. National Rifle Association, Crimestrike Crime Facts bulletin, Washington, DC, Phoenix, AZ: 1993.
2. Presentation by Lawson Lamar, Orange/Osceola (Florida) County Attorney's Office, Spring 1992.

CHAPTER 1
1. National Victim Center, Crime Clock bulletin, Arlington, VA., New York, NY: 1995.
2. Ibid.
3. U.S. Department of Commerce, Statistical Abstract of the United States, Washington DC: 1994.
4. Ibid.
5. U.S. Department of Justice, Federal Bureau of Investigation, Uniform Crime Report, Washington, DC: 1992.
6. Rep. Bill McCollum, The McCollum Report, U.S. House of Representatives, Eighth District-Florida: Fall, 1993.

CHAPTER 2
1. Nancy Myer-Czetli and Steve Czetli, *Silent Witness* (New York, NY: Birch Lane Press [Carol Publishing Group], 1993).
2. Horace O. Duke, *Where Is God When Bad Things Happen?* (St. Meinrad, IN: Abbey Press, 1991).
3. American Psychiatric Association, 5th Edition. 2013. Diagnostic and Statistical Manual of Mental Disorders. Arlington, VA: American Psychiatric Association.

4. Stanton E. Samenow, Ph.D., *Inside the Criminal Mind* (New York, NY: Time Books [Random House, Inc.], 1984).

5. Ibid.

6. Robert K. Ressler and Tom Shachtman, *Whoever Fights Monsters* (New York, NY: St. Martin's Press, 1992).

7. William H. Reid, M.D., M.P.H. and Michael G. Wise, M.D., *Diagnostic and Statistical Manual of Mental Disorders*, Third Edition, Revised (New York, NY: Brunner/Mazel Inc., 1989).

8. Rabbi Harold S. Kushner, *When Bad Things Happen to Good People* (New York, NY: Avon Books [Hearst Corporation], 1981).

CHAPTER 4

1. Marilyn Willett Heavilin, *Roses in December* (San Bernardino, CA: Here's Life Publishers, 1986).

2. Victor Frankl, *Man's Search for Meaning* (Boston, MA: Beacon Press, 1963).

CHAPTER 5

1. Levenson, Bob. "Cox Receives Death for '78 Fatal Beating." Orlando Sentinel. October 1, 1988. http://articles. orlandosentinel.com/1988-10-01/news/0070230017_1_ zellers-cox-conrad (accessed April 20, 2017).

2. Jim Leusner, "Rolling's Life Holds Clues to Killings," *Orlando Sentinel*, February 20, 1994.

3. Rick Badie and Lauren Ritchie, "Police Charge 2 Men in Slaying, Rape in Ocala Forest," *Orlando Sentinel*, February 22, 1994.

4. Robert K. Ressler and Tom Shachtman, *Whoever Fights Monsters* (New York, NY: St. Martin's Press, 1992).

5. Rep. Bill McCollum, The McCollum Report, U.S. House of Representatives, Eighth District-Florida: Fall 1993.

6. National Rifle Association, Crimestrike Crime Facts bulletin Washington, DC, Phoenix, AZ: 1993.

CHAPTER 7
1. Rapha Southeast, Depression: Insights bulletin, Atlanta, GA: 1991.
2. Ibid.

CHAPTER 8
1. Charles R. Swindoll, *Contagious Christianity* (Anaheim, CA: Insight for Living, 1993).
2. Albert Ellis, *Reason and Emotion in Psychotherapy* (New York: Lyle Stuart, 1962).
3. National Rifle Association, Crimestrike Crime Facts bulletin, Washington DC, Phoenix, AZ: 1993.
4. Allen Palmeri, "The Perfect Season," *Sports Spectrum* (Grand Rapids, MI: Discovery House Publishers), September 1994.
5. Ibid.
6. Victor Frankl, *Man's Search for Meaning* (Boston, MA: Beacon Press, 1963).

CHAPTER 9
1. Jansen, Bart. "Failure to Find Malaysia Airlines Flight 370 Leaves Many Questions Unanswered." USA Today. January 17, 2017. https://www.usatoday.com/story/news/2017/01/17/failure-find-malaysia-airlines-flight-370-leaves-many-questions-unanswered/96677490/ (accessed April 20, 2017). "Malaysia Air flight 370", South China Post Online, May 22, 2017
2. Lt. Gen. Harold G. Moore (Ret.) and Joseph L. Galloway, *We Were Soldiers Once... And Young* (New York, NY: Harper Perennial [HarperCollins Publishers, Inc.], 1993).
3. Latson, Jennifer. "Black Dahlia Murder Case Hits 68 Years Unsolved." Time.com. January 15, 2015. http://time.com/3657606/black-dahlia-murder-case/ (accessed April 20, 2017). "Top 10 Unsolved Cases", Time Magazine Online

4.   Dr. James Dobson, *When God Doesn't Make Sense* (Wheaton, IL: Tyndale House Publishers, Inc., 1993).

CHAPTER 10

1.   National Rifle Association, Crimestrike Crime Facts bulletin, Washington, DC, Phoenix AZ, 1993.
2.   Ibid.
3.   Richard Lucayo, "A Slap for a Broken Head," *Time*, November 1, 1993.
4.   Harris, Janelle. "Menendez Brothers: Everything You Need to Know." Rollingstone.com. October 2, 2016. http://www.rollingstone.com/culture/news/menendez-brothers-everything-you-need-to-know-w442897 (accessed April 20, 2017). "Menendez Brothers: Everything You Need to Know", Rolling Stone Magazine Online
5.   Dr. James Dobson, Focus on the Family newsletter, Colorado Springs, CO, September 1994.
6.   Parents of Murdered Children bulletin, Cincinnati, OH, Fall 1994.
7.   American Victim Center, "America Speaks Out: Citizens' Attitudes about Victims' Rights and Violence," Fort Worth, TX: National Victim Center, 1991.
8.   Dr. James Dobson, Focus on the Family newsletter, Colorado Springs, CO, September, 1994.

CHAPTER 11

1.   James Autry, "Love and Profit: The Art of Caring Leadership" (video), Excellence in Training Corp., 1994.

BIBLIOGRAPHY

American Psychiatric Association, 5th Edition. 2013. *Diagnostic and Statistical Manual of Mental Disorders.* Arlington, VA: American Psychiatric Association.

American Victim Center. *"America Speaks Out: Citizens' Attitudes about Victims' Rights and Violence".* Fort Worth, TX: National Crime Victim Center, 1991.

Autry, James. *Love and Profit: The Art of Caring Leadership* (video), Excellence in Training Corp, 1994.

Badie, Rick and Ritchie, Lauren. "Police Charge 2 Men in Slaying, Rape in Ocala Forest." *Orlando Sentinel,* February 22, 1994.

Crimestrike Crime Facts bulletin, Washington DC and Phoenix, AZ: National Rifle Association, 1993.

Depression Insights bulletin, Atlanta, GA: Rapha Southeast, 1991.

Dobson, Dr. James. *Focus on the Family* newsletter, Colorado Springs, CO: Focus on the Family Ministries, September, 1994.

Dobson, Dr. James. 1993. *When God Doesn't Make Sense*. Wheaton, IL: Tyndale House Publishers, Inc.

Duke, Horace O. 1991. *Where is God When Bad Things Happen?* St. Meinrad, IN: Abbey Press.

Ellis, Albert. 1962. *Reason and Emotion in Psychotherapy*. New York, NY: Lyle Stuart.

Frankl, Victor. 1963. *Man's Search for Meaning*. Boston, MA: Beacon Press.

Harris, Janelle. 2016. *Rollingstone.com*. October 2. Accessed April 20, 2017. http://www.rollingstone.com/culture/news/menendez-brothers-everything-you-need-to- know-w442897.

Jansen, Bart. 2017. *USA Today*. January 17. Accessed April 20, 2017. https://www.usatoday.com/story/news/2017/01/17/failure-find-malaysia-airlines-flight- 370-leaves-many-questions-unanswered /96677490/.

Kushner, Rabbi Harold S. 1981. *When Bad Things Happen to Good People*. New York, NY: Avon Books (Hearst Corporation).

Lamar, Lawson. conference presentation. "Crime in Orange Counrty FL." Orange/Osceola County Attorney's Office. Spring, 1992.

Latson, Jennifer. 2015. *Time.com*. January 15. Accessed April 20, 2017. http://time.com/3657606/black-dahlia-murder-case/.

Leusner, Jim. "Rolling's Life Holds Clues to Killings". *Orlando Sentinel,* February 20, 1994.

Levenson, Bob. 1988. *Orlando Sentinel*. October 1. Accessed April 20, 2017. http://articles.orlandosentinel.com/1988-10-01/news/0070230017_1_zellers-cox-conrad.

Lucayo, Richard. "A Slap for a Broken Head". *Time,* November 1, 1993.

McCollum, Rep. Bill. *The McCollum Report*. Washington DC, U.S. House of Representatives, Eighth District, FL, Fall 1993.

Moore, Harold G, Lt. Gen (Retired) and Galloway, Joseph L. 1993. *We Were Soldiers Once . . . And Young.* New York, NY: HarperPerrrennial (HarperCollins Publishers, Inc).

Myer-Czetli, Nancy and Czetli, Steve. 1993. *Silent Witness.* New York, NY: Birch Lane Press (Carol Publishing Group).

National Rifle Association, *Crimestrike Crime Facts bulletin*, Washington, DC, Phoenix, AZ: 1993.

National Victim Center, *Crime Clock* bulletin. Arlington, VA; New York, NY: 1995.

Palmeri, Allen. "The Perfect Season." *Sports Spectrum*. Grand Rapids, MI: Discovery House Publishers, September, 1994.

Parents of Murdered Children bulletin, Cincinatti, OH: Parents of Murdered Children, 1994.

Ressler, Robert K. and Shachtman, Tom. 1992. *Whoever Fights Monsters*. New York, NY: St. Martins Press.

Samenow, Stanton E., Ph.D. 1984. *Inside the Criminal Mind*. New York, NY: Time Books (Random House, Inc.).

Statistical Abstract of the United States. Washington DC: U.S. Department of Commerce, 1994.

Swindoll, Charles R. 1993. *Contagious Christianity*. Anaheim, CA: Insight for Living.

Uniform Crime Report. Washington, DC: U.S. Department of Justice, Federal Bureau of Investigation, 1992.

William H. Reid, M.D., M.P.H. and Michael G. Wise, M.D., *Diagnostic and Statistical Manual of Mental Disorders*,

Third Edition, Revised (New York, NY: Brunner/Mazel Inc., 1989).

Willett Heavilin, Marilyn. 1986. *Roses in December*. San Bernardino, CA: Here's Life Publishers.

DIRECTORY OF GRIEF SUPPORT ORGANIZATIONS

Bereaved Survivors of Homicide, Inc.
P.O. Box 561313
Orlando, FL, 32856-1313
407-254-7248

Crisis Management Group
Echo Bridge Office Park
381 Elliot Street, Ste. 180L
Newton Upper Falls, MA, 02464
617-969-0617

Families and Friends of Missing Persons & Violent Crime Victims
5023 Claremont Way
Everett, WA, 98203
425-252-6081

Mothers Against Drunk Drivers (M.A.D.D.)
511 E. John Carpenter Freeway, Ste. 700
Irving, TX, 75062
877-ASK-MADD

National Crime Victims' Research & Treatment Center
Medical University of South Carolina
67 President Street, MSC 861

2nd Floor, 10P South Building
Charleston, SC, 29425
803-792-2945

National Organization for Victim Assistance
510 King Street, Ste. 424
Alexandria, VA, 22314
800-TRY-NOVA

National Victim Centers
2000 M Street NW, Ste. 480
Washington DC, 20036
202-467-8700

Office for Victims of Crime
810 Seventh Street NW
Washington DC, 20531
800-363-0441

Parents of Murdered Children
4960 Ridge Ave, Ste. 2
Cincinnati, OH, 45209
513-721-5683

State of South Carolina, Office of the Governor, Division of Victim
Assistance
1205 Pendleton Street
Columbia, SC, 29201
803-734-1900

The Compassionate Friends
P.0. Box 3696
Oak Brook, IL, 60522
877-969-0010

Additional Praise for *The Shadow of Evil*

Jeff provides in this book a personal witness, a spiritual journey, and an informational overview of human life when encountering a tremendous tragedy and loss. A gripping account of personal violence, crucial to anyone attempting to cope emotionally, spiritually, and intellectually with their own tragedy.

Thomas T. Graff, PhD, PhD, licensed psychologist

Author Jeffrey M. Davis offers the compassion of a fellow sufferer and the no-nonsense advice of a grief counselor . . . His honest questions and the conclusion he reaches will help victims and survivors confront their doubts. Written for the layman in a vivid and readable style, Davis book offers insights and information to assist survivors in the continuing process of recovery.

Judith Inman, BA, freelance writer, *Family Violence and Sexual Assault Bulletin* Longview, TX

Your book impacted me and affected my view of the surviving victims. It has provided insight into the spiritual struggles that loved ones experience. *The Shadow of Evil* provides a resource to help understand and to treat those who have been touched by violent crime with compassion and understanding.

Gary E. Steed, former Sedgwick County (KS) sheriff

It is an emotionally binding story. I know of no other book embracing this problem from a Christian's viewpoint.

Al Allen, *Christian Standard*, Casper, WY

I review over 60 books a year. Few seem to rip apart my defenses and rub my heart with new comfort and hope as do the words of this author... This book is about violent death. Don't let that limit your choice in reading this book. It is about the violent feelings that surround loss, the agitation that faith and religious beliefs often become, and the merging of both... to move into some new moment or glimpse of healing.

Richard B. Gilbert, AB, MDiv, FAAGC, CPBC
Founding director, Connections-Spiritual Links, Valparaiso, IN

This resource brings self-understanding to survivors and teaches the rest of us how to respond to those who have experienced the horror of violence. I was moved to finish this book in one evening. This book should be required reading for law enforcement, the judiciary, the clergy and all service providers.

Greta Snitkin, co-founder, Orlando Bereaved Survivors of Homicide, Inc.

The Shadow of Evil by Jeff Davis is not only a good read, but it gives you a deep insight into the tragic death of an innocent woman and the struggle that her son went through as a Christian to reconcile what happened with his faith in God. Mr. Davis shares his innermost thoughts in a manner that will assist crime victims and their families as they attempt to understand why tragic things happen to good people and how they can find peace with themselves and with God.

Lawson Lamar, former Orange/Osceola (Florida) state attorney

The book expands beyond his (the author's) own story in an effort to reach others whose lives have been touched by violence.

Susan Rife, book reviewer, the *Wichita Eagle*

This book is terrific! Makes you think from beginning to end.

Clifford Kelley, American Management Association author, retired aerospace executive

This book is a must, primarily for victims, but also for those friends of victims who are looking for that 'right thing to say', or for a way to offer comfort to those we love. As I read the book, I found the answers to so many questions I'd been struggling with.

William C. Wise, former corporate training manager
Lockheed Martin Corporation, Bethesda, MD

ABOUT THE AUTHOR

Jeffrey M. Davis has an extensive professional background, having been in the work world since the early 1970s. His career accomplishments include serving as a law enforcement officer in Lenexa, Kansas, and Fort Worth, Texas; working in the defense industry for Boeing and Lockheed Martin; consulting as an independent management training and leadership development specialist; and working as an administrator in the field of higher education in post-secondary educational institutions. Jeff has an earned M.Ed. in the field of counseling psychology and has taught classes in numerous disciplines of psychology.

Since authoring the first edition of *The Shadow of Evil: Where Is God in a Violent World?*, Jeff has traveled extensively across the county to present to survivor groups, including the Bereaved Survivors of Homicide, Parents of Murdered Children, National Organization for Victim Assistance, and They Help Each Other Spiritually.

Jeff has a passion for victims and their unique circumstances, so he shares his personal story of the loss of his mother to the BTK serial killer as a means of building a connection between other survivors and himself. As *The Shadow of Evil* goes into its second edition, Jeff hopes his book will continue to provide comfort and solace to anyone who has suffered loss and heartache in their lives. His message is simple: no matter how overwhelming the pain today, there is a road to emotional and spiritual recovery, and therefore cause for hope after all.

Jeff is semi-retired and currently lives with his wife, Monie, and their faithful schnauzer, Paxton, in northern Colorado.

He can be reached by email at cedars51@gmail.com

CPSIA information can be obtained
at www.ICGtesting.com
Printed in the USA
LVHW071608170219
607810LV00032B/412/P